IMAGES OF

KENT AT WAR
1939-1945

RARE PHOTOGRAPHS FROM WARTIME ARCHIVES

Mark Khan

Pen & Sword
MILITARY

First published in Great Britain in 2014 by
PEN & SWORD MILITARY
An imprint of
Pen & Sword Books Ltd
47 Church Street
Barnsley
South Yorkshire
S70 2AS

ISBN 978-1-78346-346-6

Typeset by Concept, Huddersfield, West Yorkshire HD4 5JL.
Printed and bound in England by Page Bros, Norwich.

Pen & Sword Books Ltd incorporates the imprints of Pen & Sword Archaeology, Atlas, Aviation, Battleground, Discovery, Family History, History, Maritime, Military, Naval, Politics, Railways, Select, Social History, Transport, True Crime, and Claymore Press, Frontline Books, Leo Cooper, Praetorian Press, Remember When, Seaforth Publishing and Wharncliffe.

For a complete list of Pen & Sword titles please contact
PEN & SWORD BOOKS LIMITED
47 Church Street, Barnsley, South Yorkshire, S70 2AS, England
E-mail: enquiries@pen-and-sword.co.uk
Website: www.pen-and-sword.co.uk

Contents

Introduction

All images featured in this book are from the War and Peace Collection Photo Archive. Selecting 150 images for this book has proven quite a difficult exercise. The images represent many facets of life in Kent during the Second World War, but not every aspect is covered. The subject matter is driven by the available images, so some subject areas are lightly covered or, in some instances, not covered at all. This is no intentional slight, but purely based on the images available in the archive. From what was available, the quality of the images made the selection of a representative sample difficult. I hope I have done justice to the archive as a whole and commend people to look at the other images available. All the images have been digitised and are available to view free online via the Kent Photo Archive website (http://www.kentphotoarchive.com). The images cover a wide range of subjects and were taken over a timeframe that is believed to cover the period 1932–1963. The images are known to have been predominantly taken in Kent. For some the precise information is unknown. The archive would welcome any information from readers who may be able to help fill in the gaps or correct any inaccuracies in the current understanding regarding the information relating to the images.

After each image caption, the individual photo archive reference is listed. Please use this number to access or when referring to the images on the archive website.

I would like to thank Rex Cadman for allowing me the opportunity to write this book. It has been a fascinating project and I have enjoyed immensely the process of selecting, collating, researching and creating the content for this book.

My special thanks also go to Roger Smoothy, who is responsible for doing the work to make the images available online and has done much research into the history of many of the photographs, resulting in the caption that accompanies each image. Roger also made the images available for publication by extracting the archive and kindly sending them on to me.

Chapter One

The Early Years

The Start of the War

At the beginning of the Second World War, in Kentish cities, towns and villages there were still many tangible legacies of the Great War that had only ended twenty-one years previously. In November 1916 the War Trophies Committee was formed, its terms of reference being 'to deal with all questions in regard to the distribution of trophies and watch the interests of the Imperial War Museum'. A committee was formed comprising of individuals representing British and Commonwealth countries to distribute these war trophies. The word 'trophy' was defined as 'including all articles of captured enemy equipment, but such articles that were only to be considered as trophies for distribution during the war, if unserviceable or not required for conversion'. A large number of trophies, especially guns, had rival claimants, and the rule was laid down that in such cases, claims for trophies would be decided by the War Office. When a claim had been substantiated, the proviso was that it went to a Regimental Depot, a recognized public body, or a museum. Some 3,595 guns, 15,044 machine guns, 75,824 small arms and 7,887 other trophies were distributed. Large numbers of applications were received for allotment from county authorities, mayors and corporations of cities and towns, urban and parish councils, and other communities. The Committee decided that allotment of the trophies to which no formal claim within the recognised parameters had been substantiated, would be decided in conjunction with the Lord Lieutenant of the county. Many of these war trophies were allocated to various cities, towns and villages in Kent, one example of which was the village of Yalding where a German 7.7cm Feldkanone 16 was displayed in the High Street.

After the war, the Treasury donated 264 British tanks to towns that had raised money for the war effort. Tank '131' was allocated to Royal Tunbridge Wells. It was placed outside the old post office, but time, rust and the need for scrap metal during World War Two, led to its removal. A number of towns around the country, including Canterbury, Maidstone and Folkestone also received tanks.

Remarkably the only survivor of these tanks still resides in Ashford. Mark IV tank 245 was presented to the town in August 1919 by Captain Ferrar of the Army Council, in recognition of the people's generous response to the National War Savings Appeals.

(*Above*) A German 150mm sFH 13 L/14 Howitzer made by Krupp c.1915. Battery Point Sandgate. (*WanPs-2482*)

(*Opposite above*) A German 7.7cm Feldkanone 16 displayed in the Yalding High Street photographed from the B2010 looking north east, c.1935. The village of Yalding has another link with the First World War – one of the famous war poets Edmund Blunden lived in the village before the war. He volunteered for war service, joined the 11th Batallion, Royal Sussex Regiment, served in France and was awarded the Military Cross. (*WanPs-3758*)

(*Opposite below*) This photograph shows the contrast of old and new. Rochester Castle with its keep built in Norman times, contrasting with the war souvenir mounted in its grounds on a plinth on the right of the photograph: the barrel and recuperator mechanism of German First World War 7.7cm Feldkanone 96 neuer Art (7.7cm FK 96 n.A.). (*WanPs-3642*)

Evacuees in Kent

With the advent of German bombing, many children from London were evacuated to Kent. By April 1940, the Kent Education Committee reported that the number of evacuees attending elementary schools in the county was 11,498. This figure was down from 17,483 in November 1939. Whilst many individual children were evacuated to Kent, in some instances entire schools were relocated. An example of this was Kings Warren LCC School in Plumstead, which relocated to Maidstone, where it shared the new buildings of the Maidstone Grammar School. As the German bombing campaign developed in 1940, Maidstone became a target. Between July and October 1940, fifty-three people died as a result of German bombing. The worst day for casualties was 27 September 1940, subsequently named 'Black Friday', when twenty-two people were killed in as little as two minutes during the attack. In another incident a single bomber appeared from the clouds over Mill Street on 31 October 1940 and dropped its bombs killing six people in the immediate area. The increase in bombing of Maidstone eventually necessitated the evacuation of some children, with some actually returning to London.

(*Opposite page*) This photograph shows Dorothy Harris aged 6, with her two dolls Jimmy and Pongo waiting to be evacuated at Maidstone station in 1940. (*WanPs-0037*)

(*Below*) Children awaiting evacuation at Maidstone West Station, c.1940. (*WanPs-0186*)

Children being evacuated from what is believed to be Maidstone West Station, c.1940. (WanPs-0036)

Dunkirk: June 1940

On 10 May 1940 Hitler's armies struck westwards across Europe. Within three weeks Holland and Belgium had surrendered and the German Army had driven a wedge between the British and French armies. The British Expeditionary Force (BEF) and a substantial number of French troops were trapped in a diminishing pocket of land centred on the port of Dunkirk. On 25 May, Boulogne was captured and on the following day Calais fell. That evening the Admiralty signalled the start of Operation Dynamo – the evacuation of the troops stranded on the beaches at Dunkirk. The County of Kent would play a major part in the evacuation. Thousands of men were disembarked in the Port of Dover and the Southern Railway helped evacuate the tired and battered men evacuated from the Dunkirk beaches. They received help and kindness from the people of Kent as they stopped at stations and were fed and watered. The Women's Voluntary Service (WVS) opened canteens at many stations. Trains arrived at the rate of six an hour. Arrangements were made with the Post Office for the despatch of postcards which men left as they passed through. WVS members and local people helped to send thousands of these postcards to the relatives of soldiers, letting them know that they were safe. On 14 June 1940, the Secretary of State for War, Oliver Stanley, issued an official thanks to the people of Kent as a result of this:

The Dunkirk Evacuation Official Thanks to Kent

The Secretary of State for War desires to thank most sincerely those citizens who on the occasion of the return of B.E.F. personnel to this country, so generously undertook, at their own expense, to despatch from railway stations at which troops trains had halted, telegrams, letters, and postcards to the men's homes announcing their safe arrival in this country.

Sir Auckland Geddes, Regional Commissioner, South-Eastern Region, and the General Officer Commanding the troops in Kent have expressed their great appreciation of splendid help given by the people of Kent in the evacuation of the B.E.F.

A key part was played by Dover Command. In June 1940 the Admiralty issued a statement:

The Board of The Admiralty congratulate all concerned in the successful evacuation of the British Expeditionary Force and the soldiers of the Allied Armies from the Dunkirk area.

Their lordships also realize that the success was only rendered possible by the great effort made by all shore establishments, and in particular by the Dover Command, who were responsible for the organisation and direction of this difficult operation.

Amongst the fleet of little ships was an array of other types of ships. One of these iconic ships was the Paddle Steamer *Medway Queen*. She was built at Troon in 1924 specially for the New Medway Steam Packet Company for operation on the River Medway. During the 1920s and 1930s she transported holiday makers on excursions from the Medway Towns.

The P.S. *Medway Queen* was called up for war service in the autumn of 1939. Her black, white and cream peacetime livery was changed to battleship grey, armament was fitted, modifications were made to fit minesweeping gear and she became HMS *Medway Queen*.

She spent the early part of the 1940s patrolling the Straits of Dover. On 27 May 1940 she received orders to head to the beaches of Dunkirk to help embark troops of the BEF. The *Medway Queen* continued to evacuate troops until Monday, 3 June.

She was one of the first vessels to reach the beaches and she was one of the last to leave. As a result of actions during the Dunkirk evacuation several of her crew were decorated for bravery. Overall she is credited with rescuing over 7,000 men, and also with having shot down three German aircraft. Damaged by a collision during the evacuation, she limped into Dover harbour, where she was welcomed by the sound of the sirens from all the ships in the harbour and a signal from Vice Admiral Ramsey: 'Well Done Medway Queen'. After the war, she returned to operation with her original owners, the Medway Steam Packet Company, providing excursions once again to the seaside resorts of Southend and Herne Bay. The *Medway Queen* is still in existence today, being owned by the New Medway Steam Packet Company Ltd.

The *Medway Queen* at Chatham, c.1950. Returned to her civilian livery, she is once more taking holiday makers on summer excursions – a very different role to that which she played only five years previously. (WanPs-1739)

The artist W.O. Miller painting *The End of Dunkirk*. (*WanPs-0156*)

Invasion Defences

After the withdrawal from Dunkirk, the threat of German invasion seemed inevitable. The Kent coast was the nearest part of mainland Great Britain to the coast of mainland Europe and desparately needed to be defended. Initially, simple improvised defences were set up. Pillboxes, anti-tank fortifications, gun emplacements and an array of defensive fortifications began to appear around the county's landscape. Key points in the defensive plan, such as Canterbury, Maidstone, Chatham and the Royal Military Canal, became heavily fortified. In July 1940 stop-lines were set up to divide England into several small defended areas surrounded by anti-tank obstacles which were planned to be strongly defended using natural landscape features. Pillboxes formed a major part of the Second World War defensive strategy of Britain. This strategy was created by General Sir Edmund Ironside and led to the setting up of networks of pillboxes which were constructed to house machine guns and anti-tank guns, and to provide maximum protection to those who manned these structures. The lines of defence followed points of weakness and strategic importance such as coastal areas, railways, roads, canals and rivers. The design of the structures made use of shuttered concrete construction techniques, and so the buildings were quick, easy and cheap to build – essential qualities in wartime.

On 25 June 1940, General Paget, Chief of Staff to the Commander-in-Chief Home Forces, submitted General Ironside's anti-invasion plan to the War Cabinet. As a result of this, a number of defensive networks were set up in Kent. The defensive line became known as 'Ironside's Line'.

A pillbox at a railway bridge near the A20 at Westwell Leacon. It is believed that this pillbox formed part of the defences specifically designed to protect the nearby Maidstone to London railway line. The defences here comprised two 'Type 24' pillboxes: six-sided structures with one doorway, flanked by two windows. The remaining walls included a central window providing all-round visibility. These structures were demolished as part of the construction of the Channel Tunnel Rail Link, the new line running parallel to the existing rail line. The site here was formally recorded prior to demolition to ensure that the historical details were not lost – part of the remit of the Channel Tunnel Rail Link project. (WanPs-0344)

A temporary roadblock set up somewhere in Kent, using an old lorry and a makeshift barrier, c.1940. *(WanPs-0073)*

Barbed wire defences at Ashford, with 4ft reinforced concrete cubes, often referred to as 'pimples'. *(WanPs-0225)*

A disguised pillbox located at Western Undercliff, St Lawrence, Ramsgate. This pillbox formed part of the coastal defences at Pegwell Bay. Most of the western undercliff has been extensively redeveloped since the war; the bathing huts here have long since disappeared. *(WanPs-0346)*

War-time Scrap Drives

Throughout the war there was a focus on utilising scrap metal as salvage. In July 1940, an appeal led to members of the public donating thousands of tons of aluminium to help the war effort. The appeal for pots and pans and other aluminium household articles in July 1940, the collection of aluminium from fallen German aircraft, and the careful sorting and melting of manufacturers' scrap yielded a substantial amount. Virtually all of the output of aluminium was absorbed for aircraft and naval construction. The WVS helped with collecting the donated metal by setting up receiving centres and organising collections.

At one such centre in Hythe the following conversation was recorded between a centre organiser and a small boy who had brought along some aluminium pots and pans: 'And are all these pans you've brought to be made into a bomber?' The small boy retorted, 'rather not – into a FIGHTER'

A second major scrap drive was launched in 1942, this time for iron and steel. The entry of Japan into the war had meant the supply of steel from America reduced significantly as it was now needed by the Americans themselves. It was recognised that enormous quantities of scrap metal were still available in Great Britain. A plan to collect 43,000 tons per week was issued by the Ministry of Supply.

Throughout the country people everywhere responded to this initiative by looking for and collecting scrap metal. Much of this was metal being used for 'non-essential purposes'. In Royal Tunbridge Wells one such location where metal was removed was from Woodbury Park cemetery where many of the handsome wrought iron railings and chains marking out family graves were removed. An indignant letter from a Tunbridge Wells local, W.C. Cripps the younger, dated July 1942, demanded 'compensation from the Council for the damage done by clumsy workmen' to the kerbstones of his family's grave – these had just been restored – when the railings were removed as scrap to make munitions. It is understood that Mr Cripps, being both a lawyer and former town clerk, got his compensation.

This photograph shows scrap metal being collected for the war effort in Tunbridge Wells. *(WanPs-2413)*

(*Above*) Another shot showing the Tunbridge Wells Borough Council road roller No. 8097 crushing scrap metal outside the Medway Coal Company Depot. (*WanPs-0139*)

(*Opposite above*) Another photograph showing scrap metal being collected in Tunbridge Wells. In this image some iron railings are being removed. (*WanPs-2414*)

(*Opposite below*) Crushing scrap metal collected for the war effort. This photograph was taken in front of the Medway Coal Company Depot at 160 St James Road, Tunbridge Wells, c.1941. The road roller No. 8097 was built in Kent by Aveling & Porter in 1913 and still exists today, beautifully restored, named Moby Dick, and painted in the colours of Tunbridge Wells Borough Council. (*WanPs-2523*)

Chapter Two

The Kent Home Guard

On the evening of Tuesday 14 May 1940 The Secretary for War, Anthony Eden, issued an appeal for volunteers to defend against the expected threat of invasion by German parachute forces:

We want large numbers of such men in Great Britain, who are British subjects, between the ages of 17 and 65, to come forward now and offer their services in order to make assurance doubly sure. The name of the new Force which is now to be raised will be 'The Local Defence Volunteers'. You will form part of the armed forces, and your period of service will be for the duration of the war. You will not be paid, but you will receive uniform and will be armed. You will be entrusted with certain vital duties for which reasonable fitness and a knowledge of firearms is necessary. In order to volunteer, what you have to do is to give in your name at your local police station; and then, as and when we want you, we will let you know. This appeal is directed chiefly to those who live in country parishes, in small towns, in villages and in less densely inhabited suburban areas. I must warn you that for certain military reasons there will be some localities where the numbers required will be small, and others where your services will not be required at all. Here, then, is the opportunity for which so many of you have been waiting. Your loyal help, added to the arrangements which already exist, will make and keep our country safe.

Around the country thousands came forward to volunteer. In the county of Kent, this appeal was enthusiastically embraced. In Dover over twenty people had given their names by 8.00am on the following day. On the Wednesday throughout the day there was a steady stream of volunteers arriving at the police station to register. It was reported that volunteers were of all classes but included a retired general and several officers. By Friday, 17 May, over 400 men had signed up.

The LDV eventually became better known as the Home Guard. In Kent, forty battalions were eventually formed. The Kent Home Guard also formed units that manned coastal defences and anti-aircraft defences.

Kent Home Guard battalions, as of 1944:

1. Ashford
2. Charing
3. Canterbury
4. St. Augustine's
5. Wingham
6. Thanet

7. Lyminge	13. Rochester	20. Sevenoaks
8. Cinque Ports	14. Hoo	21. Tonbridge
9. Faversham	16. Gravesend	22. Tunbridge Wells
10. Sittingbourne	17. Northfleet	23. Goudhurst
11. Maidstone	18. Dartford	24. Malling
12. Chatham	19. Farningham	

The following battalions were utility battalions raised by major industries in Kent:

25. GPO	28. 1st Southern Railway	31. Dockyard (Chatham)
26. Kent Bus	29. Mid-Kent	32. Edenbridge
27. Kent Electric	30. Sheppey	33. Short Brothers

The following seven battalions were part of the London zone, but were also included as part of the Kent Home Guard:

51. Bromley	54. Chislehurst	57. Sidcup
52. Farnborough	55. Beckenham	
53. Orpington	56. Erith	

An example of one of the Home Guard Units was No.3 Company of the Cinque Ports Battalion located in Dover and which had become fully established by the end of August 1940, and published orders for the week in the local newspaper *The Dover and East Kent News*. A sample of the weekly orders for 23 August 1940 is recorded below:

HOME GUARD
CINQUE PORTS BATTALION

No. 3 Company

Orders for week ending 31st August 1940, by Capt. W. Moore, Commander.
Officer of the week: Platoon Officer Doyle.
No. 11 Platoon – Parade on Monday. 7pm to 8pm, for instructional purposes.
Section leaders please note.
Recruits – All recruits who have not yet passed their test to parade under instructors on Monday, Wednesday and Friday, at the Drill Hall at 7pm, and on Tuesday, Thursday and Saturday, to report to their section leaders at their Platoon HQ from 9pm to 10.30pm, for guard duties, etc.
"N" Platoon – A Platoon of No. 3 Company has been formed at the Dockyard for Admiralty establishments at Dover. Mr G.S. Henderson is Platoon Officer and Mr M.W. McGrath, Assistant Platoon Officer.

Light Automatics-Platoon Commanders to submit the name of a man with special training in Light Automatics. He should be available for duty every night, and will probably have to undergo a short course. Travelling and subsistence allowance will be paid.

Notices – Members of the Company have been elected honorary members of the Buffs Club at the Drill Hall, Shellons Street, Folkestone, and the Friendly Societies Club, Biggin St., Dover.

It is hoped that members of the Home Guard will support the concert to be held at the Town Hall on Monday in aid of the "Spitfire" Fund.

(Signed) M.G. Lohan, Second-in-Command and Adjutant

The Kent Home Guard continued to serve throughout the war, fulfilling an important role. They trained hard and much of this training was as dangerous as that carried out by any regular army unit. On occasions fatal accidents occurred.

In June 1942 Capel Home Guard member Charles Arthur Holman was fatally injured at Alkham, near Capel le Ferne, whilst taking part in a live firing exercise. Charles Holman had recently joined the Home Guard and was married with two young children. The exercise involved the Home Guard troops being formed up in two sections, where bursts of machine gun fire would be directed near the group as part of a battle inoculation exercise. Four Bren guns were used, one to fire in front of the group, one to the rear and two for effect only. The guns were manned by experienced regular Army NCOs who were performing a demonstration that was carried out regularly at army battle schools. When the firing commenced one witness stated that the rounds were striking within three to four yards of the group, causing him to become alarmed. It was at this time that Charles Holman fell injured. He had been struck in the forehead by a bullet. It was acknowledged at the enquiry held after the incident that the fire was closer than intended but it would have been impossible for the victim to have received a direct hit. The accident was deemed to have been caused by an unfortunate ricochet and a verdict of accidental death concluded.

Another aspect of the defence of Great Britain after the fall of France was the forming of highly secret Auxiliary Units. These were essentially a secret resistance network of highly trained volunteers, recruited from the best members of the Home Guard, prepared to be Britain's last-ditch line of defence and operated in a network of cells from hidden underground bases around the UK. Being at the front line of a possible cross-channel attack a number of auxiliary units were formed in Kent.

A headquarters was set up at a house called the Garth near the village of Bilting, between Ashford and Canterbury. In command here was Captain Peter Fleming (the brother of the author Ian Fleming). In the woods nearby, a number of subterranean chambers were dug by the Royal Engineers. Nearby another large underground shelter was created in a large boat-shaped depression in Kings Wood. This was large enough to shelter up to 120 men.

One unit south of Faversham, whose hideout was located at Stocking Wood near Baddlesmere, found an imaginative solution to the problem of disguising the digging of a hide-out in the chalky Kent soil from air observation. The spoil was placed in a natural hole in the wood. Using explosives, a series of charges were laid in line with the spoil dump. The charges were then blown forming what then looked like a line of bomb craters from the air.

Many other Auxiliary patrols existed in Kent. Much of the story of these units still remains secret today.

As the war progressed, no doubt many of the tasks carried out by the Kent Home Guard became tedious and repetitive. For many they were carried out in conjunction with other occupations. Hours of training and guard duty were carried out. It is said however that the Kent Home Guard never lost the 'Spirit of 1940'. The Home Guard was eventually stood down on 1 November 1944.

These men of the Kent Home Guard are receiving instruction with their .30-06 Model 1917 rifles. Britain received large numbers of these rifles from the United States. They were chambered for the American .30-06 cartridge rather than the standard British .303 round. To help differentiate these rifles as being non-standard calibre a red band was painted on the fore end of the rifle. These can be seen in this photograph just before the front swivel housing. The decision was taken to arm the Home Guard with these rifles to simplify the supply of ammunition. (WanPs-2259)

(*Above*) This photograph shows a member of the Kent Home Guard armed with his rifle and skilfully camouflaged in ghillie suit. (*WanPs-0076*)

(*Opposite above*) Another shot of the Home Guard. The man in the centre is holding a Sten Mk II sub-machine gun. (*WanPs-00179*)

(*Opposite below*) Members of the Kent Home Guard photographed in the back of a civilian lorry. They are all armed with Model 1917 .30-06 rifles. Curiously, this detachment all seem to have the front upper wood fore end removed from all their weapons. (*WanPs-2332*)

(*Above*) Members of the Kent Home Guard photographed during a training exercise in Kent. (*WanPs-2480*)

(*Opposite above*) Lieutenant-General Bernard Montgomery with members of the Home Guard. In April 1941, General Montgomery became commander of XII Corps responsible for the defence of Kent. The man in the cenre has a later issue 'reduced pattern' Home Guard armband. (*WanPs-2464*)

(*Opposite below*) Home Guard members under instruction. This group is made up of members from a number of different units, some of which are wearing Civil Defence ARP uniforms, and some the uniform of the Royal Observer Corps. (*WanPs-2272*)

(*Above*) Members of the Kent Home Guard undergoing instruction for field cooking. The sergeant performing the cooking instruction would appear to be an experienced soldier judging by the First World War medal ribbons he is wearing on his battledress. A warrant officer looks on from the left. The men observing the demonstration on the bench are wearing the cap badge of the Queen's Own Royal West Kent Regiment, the affiliated regiment for a number of the Kent Home Guard battalions. (*WanPs-2273*)

(*Opposite above*) A Kent Home Guard soldier with Mk II Sten gun. (*WanPs-0178*)

(*Opposite below*) Members of the Kent Home Guard training with their 2-pdr anti-tank guns. To accord them their proper title, these guns are Ordnance QF 2-pounder Mk IX on Carriage Mk I. They were superseded very early in the war by larger weapons in front line service. They were issued to some Home Guard Units in 1943. This series of photos was taken in Calverley Park in Tunbridge Wells. (*WanPs-0065*)

(*Above*) A second photograph of the Home Guard exercise in Calverley Park, Tunbridge Wells. (*WanPs-0066*)

(*Opposite above*) The third photograph of the Home Guard exercise in Calverley Park, Tunbridge Wells. The gun is in the firing position and appears to be of great interest to the school boys of Tunbridge Wells. (*WanPs-00312*)

(*Opposite below*) The actual unit the men in this photograph belong to is unknown. They are most likely a regular unit exercising, but the photograph perhaps forms a good representation of how an Auxiliary unit may have looked. The grim-set determination of these tough-looking men shows what a German invader might have been confronted by. (*WanPs-2451*)

This image shows what is most likely regular soldiers armed with two weapons that were issued to the Home Guard. On the left the soldier is holding a Thompson model M1921 or M1928 sub-machine gun. Examples of these weapons came to the Home Guard under the unofficial scheme operated by the American Committee for the Defence of British Homes in 1940. The first weapons to actually enter British service were guns originally destined for the French Army, but as France had fallen by the time the guns were ready for shipping, they eventually ended up at Liverpool, re-directed to the French government in exile in the UK. The guns were duly appropriated by the British. The soldier on the right is holding a 0.303in Lewis Machine Gun Mark SS, originally introduced for Naval use as a 'shoulder shooting' weapon with modified shortened butt, removed radiator assembly and muzzle compensator. Owing to the shortage of machine guns after Dunkirk it was issued to both the regular army and the Home Guard as a stop-gap weapon. (WanPs-0063)

Chapter Three

Life During Wartime

Identity Cards

As war approached, preparations were made to enable a national register to be rapidly compiled and identity cards issued. Every man, woman and child had to carry an identity (ID) card at all times and the cards would include the following information:

- Name
- Sex
- Age
- Occupation, profession, trade or employment
- Address
- Marriage status
- Membership of Naval, Military or Air Force Reserves or Auxiliary Forces, or of Civil Defence Services or Reserves.

Approximately 46 million cards were issued. The card had to be produced to a policeman or member of the military on demand, or alternatively within two days at a police station. Posters were created urging people to 'Carry Your Identity Always – you may be asked for it anytime to prove to the police or military who you are and where you live.'

The *Dover Express* on Friday 14 June 1940 carried an announcement from the Registrar General 'to remind the public that the military as well as the police are now empowered to demand the production of National Registration Identity Cards. As these powers may be widely exercised in future by both the military and the police the need is emphasized for all persons over 16 to carry their identity cards about with them.'

Not everybody heeded this advice. In October 1941 Louisa Chubb was summoned to appear at Dover Police Court for failing to produce her identity card on 2 September 1941. She was given a form requiring her to produce the card in two days. This did not happen, so enquiries were made and it was ascertained that she was in fact away hop picking. The identity card was not produced until 15 September. In court she stated that she 'thought it would be alright if she did not show it'. The police looked upon these cases as very serious matters. Pleading guilty she was fined 10s with 4s costs.

Again in Dover during a weekend in November 1943 a check-up on identity cards at dances and cinemas was carried out by the police. As a result nearly 200 people were found without their identity cards. All were required to produce them at the police station within forty-eight hours. It was emphasised again in the report in the *Dover Express*, 'It cannot be too widely known that identity cards should be carried. Much unnecessary work for the police and inconvenience to the people themselves is caused by their action in leaving their identification at home.'

The Identity Card was finally abolished in February 1952.

Soldiers from the Leicestershire Regiment carrying out an identity check on the corner of the High Street and Military Road, Chatham, on 23 May 1944. The following information regarding this photo came from Maureen Tierney in July 2009. 'The lady holding the pram was my mum. Her name was Ellen May Kitney, though everyone knew her as Ethel. The two boys in the pram are my brothers, Reg who has now died, and Jackie, now 67, who lives at Borstal. The lady beside her in the glasses is my auntie Daisy Carey. I was born four years later. My mum was just 24 when that photograph was taken. She was lovely and had long dark hair. My dad bought her the little suit she is wearing. They lived in Skinner Street, Chatham, at the time. My dad, Jack Kitney, was her second husband. He worked at Ambrose's, the greengrocers off The Delce in Rochester for thirty-six years, and was three months off his 92nd birthday when he died. My mum had lots of jobs, mainly cleaning and fruit picking.' The soldier on the far left is wearing a cotton .303 ammunition bandoleer across his chest and is sporting four seniority chevrons indicating he has four years army service. *(WanPs-0033)*

A naval policeman carrying out an identity check on Military Road/High Street Chatham, 23 May 1944. *(WanPs-0169)*

A policeman performing an identity card check on the driver of the Ford Popular saloon car 'somewhere in Kent', c.1941.
(*WanPs-0262*)

An army major performing an ID check, corner of High Street and Military Road Chatham.
(*WanPs-0350*)

Wings For Victory

In October 1942 the National Savings Committee announced that a 'Wings for Victory' week campaign would be held between 5 March and 3 July 1943. This was to be based on previous appeals such as the War Weapons and Warship Weeks. The 'Wings for Victory' event was to be built around air power in general and the Royal Air Force in particular. Dover's Wings for Victory week set a target of raising £30,000, which equated to the cost of a flight of six Spitfire fighters. The week was opened by Air Vice-Marshal Basil Embry DFC AFC ADC. Embry was famous for having evaded the Germans for two months after being shot down. While making his way to Spain he was captured by the Vichy French. He escaped again and eventually arrived in Gibraltar after almost ten weeks on the run. Air Vice-Marshal Embry's link to Dover was via his father Rev J. Embry who was vicar of St Bartholomew's church (now demolished and replaced by a block of flats). The Dover Rural District Council total came in at a very successful £41,429.

Nearby Eastry District Council's Wings for Victory week appeal was also extremely successful, with the magnificent total of £142,308 2s 6d raised against a target of £80,000.

Blood Donors

Many thousands of lives were saved as a direct result of blood transfusion. During the war volunteers came forward readily to give their blood to hospitals for transfusion purposes for bomb casualties and other causes. Blood plasma could be dried and exported to all war fronts. The British public was bombarded with emotive images and appeals, to such an extent that donor responses remained defiantly high in spite of air raids. Glowing recommendations of transfusion enabled the civilian public to feel empowered in the war effort. The romantic appeal of saving the lives of men in the field served as a powerful incentive for donation. Posters were created with an image of a charging British soldier framed by a symbolic blood plasma bottle, with a banner proclaiming 'If he should fall, is your blood there to save him?'

It was yet another important national service for which the people of Kent during the war volunteered in great numbers.

(*Above*) Sticking saving stamps on a bomb for direct delivery by the RAF to Hitler in the Wings for Victory week outside the County Hotel, High Street, Canterbury. Watching on the extreme left is Private S. Butler of the Sturry Home Guard. (*WanPs-0031*)

(*Opposite page*) Two photographs of the Blood Transfusion Service donors clinic in High Street, Chatham, *c.*1941. (*WanPs-0185 & 2155*)

Blood for the Eighth Army. Eight hundred bottles of dried blood given by donors in Kent being packed into a van at Maidstone for shipment to North Africa, April 1943. (*WanPs-0269*)

Mobile Canteens

During wartime it became the legal responsibility of all employers of 200 or more workers to provide canteen facilities. The rapid de-centralisation of industry created a sudden demand for mass feeding which could not be met by ordinary means. Provision also needed to be made for the victims of air raids whose homes had been destroyed or damaged and who could not feed themselves.

The expansion of the armed forces also resulted in units being stationed in remote villages or away from main centres. These troops needed to be provided with food and sustenance. Organisations such as the Women's Voluntary Service (WVS), Young Men's Christian Association (YMCA) and the Navy, Army and Air Force Institutes (NAAFI) provided mobile refreshment wagons.

During the blitz in 1940, these mobile facilities had provided a vital service. In 1941, the Ministry of Food felt that the often ad-hoc arrangements for deploying the available mobile facilities in emergency situations requiring large numbers of people to be fed, needed backing up with more formal arrangements. As such, what was known as the 'Queens Messengers Convoys' were created. Each convoy consisted of twelve vehicles, one water tank lorry, two food storage lorries, three mobile canteens and four motorcycles. Apart from the men who drove the heavy lorries and lifted the heavy kitchen equipment from the lorries, the convoys were almost entirely staffed by approximately fifty WVS members. A convoy could feed up to 6,000 people per day.

Many of the vehicles were provided by donations from the British War Relief Society, a US-based humanitarian organisation dealing with the supply of non-military aid such as food, clothes, medical supplies and financial aid to people in Great Britain. In Kent during July 1941 one such vehicle was presented to one of the Queens

Perhaps one of the more unusual mobile canteens, based in Kent during the war. This vehicle appears to be based on a Rolls Royce vehicle. The photograph is believed to have been taken in Tunbridge Wells. (WanPs-2465)

Messengers Convoys based in Kent. The vehicle was inscribed 'To the people of Dover, from the people of Dover, Massachusetts, USA'. The vehicle was formally handed over by the head of the British War Relief Society, Mr B. de N. Cruger in London. After being inspected by the United States ambassador's wife, Mrs Winant, the vehicle was driven to Dover. The local newspaper at the time described the vehicle as being of the 'latest type to make its appearance in the country, being fully equipped with kitchen utensils, including two thermos urns, bakelite cups and soup plates, cutlery, a sink and a paraffin stove'. Its purpose was declared to be for air-raid use in Kent. These vehicles must have provided a welcome sight during wartime to those either living or stationed in Kent.

(*Opposite above*) A Royal Engineers anti-aircraft unit at a YMCA tea, car c.1941. By 1943 in Kent, the YMCA was running thirty-eight such mobile canteens. (*WanPs-0304*)

(*Opposite below*) A NAAFI tea wagon photographed at Shorne, near Gravesend providing a welcome cup of tea to the personnel of No. 23 Barrage Balloon Centre at Gravesend Airfield during 1944. This unit was deployed here as part of the Anti-diver Belt (defences against the V1 flying bombs) for the Medway Towns. These defences were made up of balloons drawn at short notice from all over the UK in June 1944. (*WanPs-2366*)

(*Below*) A WVS Queens Messenger convoy 'food flying squad' providing some welcome sustenance to what appear to be local dignitaries somewhere in Kent. (*WanPs-0258*)

A Bedford OX 30 Food Flying Squad mobile canteen. This vehicle was provided by donations from the people of Kent County, Michigan, USA, which is inscribed on the side of the vehicle. Two of the convoy's motorcycles and riders are also shown. *(WanPs-0337)*

Rationing

The first commodity to be controlled after the Second World War began in September 1939 was petrol. On 8 January 1940, bacon, butter and sugar were rationed. This was followed by successive ration schemes for meat, tea, jam, biscuits, breakfast cereals, cheese, eggs, lard, milk and canned and dried fruit.

The *Dover and East Kent Express* in January 1940 carried an advertisement from the Ministry of Food entitled 'Reasons for Rationing'. It explained that war had meant the re-planning of food supplies, the reason being that most of our bacon, butter and sugar came from overseas. Four main reasons were given for the need for rationing:

1. **The prevention of waste of food** – We must not ask our sailors to bring us unnecessary food cargoes at the risk of their lives.

2. **Increasing the war effort** – Our shipping carries food and armaments in their raw and finished state and other essential raw materials for home consumption and the export trade. To reduce our purchase of food abroad is to release ships for bringing other imports. So we strengthen our war effort.
3. **Divides supplies equally** – There will be ample supplies for our forty-four and a half million people. But we must divide them fairly, everyone being treated alike. No one must be left out.
4. **Prevents uncertainty** – Your ration book assures you of your fair share. Rationing means that there will be no uncertainty – and no queues.

During the course of the war, rationing certainly resulted in the prevention of uncertainty. Unfortunately for many people in Kent and elsewhere in the country, the promise about the prevention of queues did not!

Women queuing outside a fruit shop, Week Street, Maidstone. (*WanPs-0295*)

Women collecting ration coupons. (WanPs-0106)

Chapter Four

Soldiers in Kent

Kent has long had an association with the British Army. The county was for many years represented by two county regiments, the Queen's Own Royal West Kent Regiment whose formation dates back to 1881, and the Buffs (Royal East Kent Regiment) whose formation dates back 1751. Both regiments have gone through a number of amalgamations and are now part of the Princess of Wales Royal Regiment. The regimental depots of the Royal West Kents and the Buffs were at Maidstone and Canterbury. Another military site long associated with Kent are the firing ranges at Hythe. The Small Arms School Corps, a small corps of the British Army responsible for maintaining the proficiency of the army in the use of small arms, support weapons and range management, were located here for many years until moving to Warminster in Wiltshire in 1969.

The Territorial Army in Kent was represented by The Kent Yeomanry. This was formed in 1920 with the amalgamation of the Royal East Kent (The Duke of Connaught's Own) Yeomanry (Mounted Rifles) and West Kent Yeomanry (Queen's Own). In a similar manner to the regular Kent infantry regiments, the Yeomanry has also gone through a number of amalgamations and survives today as C (Kent & Sharpshooters Yeomanry) Sqn, part of The Royal Yeomanry.

During the Second World War, many units of many nationalities representing the Allied Armies were stationed in Kent. Initially they played the part of the County's defenders, then as the war progressed and the tide turned against the Axis forces, became part of, or supported the Allied Forces fighting in Northern Europe.

One of the Second World War's most charismatic commanders, Lieutenant-General Sir Brian Horrocks KCB KBE DSO MC, the commander of XXX Corps during its advance through Europe in 1944/45, recalls his experiences in Kent in 1941:

> I was delighted when on the 25th of June I was made an acting major-general and ordered to take over command of the 44th (Home Counties) Division. The 44th was an old-established Territorial division, whose three brigades came from Surrey (the Queen's 131st Bde), Kent (the Buffs and the West Kents 132nd Bde), and Sussex (133rd Bde) and occupied the south-eastern corner of England. I found myself therefore, responsible for what was then regarded as the

No. I German invasion area, stretching from the Isle of Thanet to Dover and on to Folkestone.

Invasion or not, it was certainly the most exciting part of England at that time. We had a grandstand view not only of the Battle of Britain, with its dog-fights over our heads, but also of the nightly naval war that went on in the Channel.

At this time the man in charge of South Eastern Command was none other than Lieutenant-General Bernard Montgomery, who would go on to become the well-known Field Marshal Montgomery. When 'Monty' had taken over South Eastern Command, he had instituted a regime of continuous training and insisted on high levels of physical fitness for both officers and other ranks. He was ruthless in sacking officers he considered would be unfit for command in action. General Horrocks describes his experiences of this after being posted to SE Command:

I had previously experienced Mongomery's training methods when I had been a brigadier in his 3rd division just after our return from Dunkirk, but even so I was unprepared for his atonishing activity as the GOC-in-C South Eastern Command. It was as though atomic bombs were exploding all over this rural corner of Britain. Before his arrival a distinctly peace-time atmosphere had prevailed. All this changed overnight.

General Montgomery immediately made changes that prevented officers and warrant officers living with their families. He reasoned that in war a soldier could not concentrate on his military training if half his mind was concerned with domestic problems.

The second major change he made was regarding physical fitness. General Horrocks goes on to explain in his autobiography that Monty believed that too many officers spent too much time in their offices and were becoming fat, almost permanently chair-borne and no good for war. Montgomery dictated that, 'Every officer in command must carry out two cross-country runs weekly, irrespective of age or rank'. Horrocks describes in his memoirs how his senior medical officer protested against this no-exception rule and mentioned a senior administrative staff officer. 'Colonel X must not run sir. If he does he will probably die.' Monty replied, 'Let him die. Much better to die now rather than in the midst of a battle when it might be awkward to find a replacement.' Colonel X did run and Colonel X didn't die.

Monty put in place a scheme of constant training exercises of every sort in South Eastern Command. He became highly respected by many that served under him. General Horrocks describes how he was regarded during his tenure as Commander in the South East:

Army Commanders with many thousands of troops under their command tend to become remote god-like characters who few know even by sight. Yet in some extraordinary way Monty's influence permeated all strata of SE Command, and his knowledge of the personalities under his command was uncanny.

Many soldiers experienced life in Kent during the war. Here is a personal recollection by Corporal Arthur Bridge who was based at Hothfield Camp near Ashford:

For a long period in 1945 I was an 18-year-old Corporal in 9th Btn the Worcestershire Regiment on Hothfield Common. The 9th Worcestershire was situated on the left hand side of the road and on the right hand side was a battalion of the Royal Warwickshires. So you had two battalions, approx 1,200 infantry soldiers, camped there. I say camped, but from a Worcestershire point of view it was a fine posting. The Nissen Huts were in good condition and all paths and in-camp roadways immaculate. There was a very good bath area, a fine Mess Hall and always plenty of hot water. The only drawback was the toilets!!! They consisted of pits, planks and canvas. I suppose they may had [sic] been but I never remember them being emptied. Things must have grown very well there for years after! I remember my time at Hothfield fondly. The countryside was lovely. Ashford in those days was a pleasant market town.

Arthur goes on to describe the importance for the soldiers based at Hothfield Camp of the local station in those days, known as Hothfield Halt:

Quite a few of the stopping trains from Charing Cross called there and to us it was an important station. This was especially so on a Sunday night when we returned from a 24 hour or 48 hour leave. More important it was an open station after a certain time at night. This was important because lots of us on 3 or 4 shillings per day had either no ticket, or ones that had run out far short of Hothfield.

The front of the camp – on the road – was a fine sight with grass well cut and the regimental badge and motto (FIRM) picked out in white stones and flowers. There was also a tall flagpole and the flag was 'bugled' up at reveille and lowed [sic] at lights out. We had some very fine buglers and had you lived there then you maybe would have not welcomed it at 6:30 in the morning. I was of course there on 8 May which was VE Day. Most of us were given a 24-hour pass. A lot of us travelled to London (back early hours to the Halt). The rest went into Ashford.

There were significant risks involved in serving on the Home Front as well as overseas. Not only was it possible to be killed by enemy action, the danger of death from accident was also high.

This is graphically illustrated as reported in the *East Kent and Dover Express* on 19 January 1945 when a live mine exploded killing twenty soldiers and severely injuring others. The *Express* reports the incident as happening at 'a camp in Kent', without giving a specific location, presumably as a result of wartime reporting restrictions, but is believed to have possibly been at Hythe. The explosion occurred inside a Nissen hut during a lesson when an instructor was giving a lecture to a class of thirty-five men, who included those recovering from wounds and undergoing a refresher course. Due to a shortage of dummy mines, the instructor Lance-Sergeant Herbert Fisher was using a live mine. A survivor, Pte Harry Bentley, explained how he had handed the mine to Sergt Fisher who had commenced to move the lever mechanism on the mine when it exploded. Pte Bentley explained that it was a mystery why the mine had detonated as he had in his hand both the cartridge and detonator, so the mine should not have functioned. Early in the inquest proceedings, the coroner had been informed that there was a live mine in the courtroom that had been brought in as evidence! The coroner on finding that a live mine was present at the proceedings, stated 'then I must ask that it is immediately taken from the room. I wish for no demonstrations with live mines here.'

From the description of the event, it seems likely this mine was a British Mk 1 or Mk 2 anti-personnel fragmentation mine. This type of mine was similar in function to the deadly German S-mine which, when initiated, was launched into the air by a propelling charge and then exploded above ground to maximise injury. A verdict of death by misadventure was recorded. It is almost inconceivable today that a live anti-personnel mine would be used for instructional purposes, let alone be brought into a court inquest. At the time however, such items were commonplace and perhaps it was a case of familiarity breeding a certain amount of contempt which contributed to this tragic accident.

Soldiers of what is believed to be the 46th Light Anti-Aircraft Regiment playing football at an unknown location in Kent, c.1940. (WanPs-0055)

The crew of a 3-inch mortar posing for the camera. The unit these men belong to is unknown. Their helmets feature unusual camouflage painting. The mortar bombs appear to be live mortar bombs – they are fitted with an early No. 150-type percussion fuse. *(WanPs-0069)*

A group of Royal West Kents photographed during Exercise Bumper in 1941. This exercise involved British and Canadian forces around East Anglia and London and surrounding area. It was designed to test the ability of British forces to destroy a German Army after invading Great Britain. *(WanPs-0075)*

(*Above*) Army radio operators training with portable No. 18 wireless sets. (*WanPs-0181*)

(*Opposite page*) Two British Army NCOs c.1942 of very different heights – no doubt posed by the photographer. Note the gas detector brassard worn by both men on the left arm. The NCO on the right also has his protective anti-gas eye shields tucked into his webbing above his right hand ammunition pouch. (*WanPs-0199*)

Troops on exercise photographed outside the Gun Hotel, Horsmonden, near Royal Tunbridge Wells. (WanPs-0205)

A Universal Carrier passes a Churchill tank, undergoing maintenance or repair, parked in front of the Vine Hotel in Goudhurst. Note the white cross painted on the side of the universal carrier, marking it as a distinct member of one of two exercising forces. (WanPs-0206)

A mixed group of army officers and civilians, photographed in what is believed to be the Lydd area. *(WanPs-0308)*

Troops practising or possibly performing a public demonstration with collapsible assault boats. The photograph is taken in Mote Park, Maidstone. *(WanPs-0320)*

(*Above*) Another photo of the troops exercising in Mote Park, Maidstone. On the banks of the lake can be seen a large audience of spectators. (*WanPs-0325*)

(*Opposite above*) A group of Royal Canadian Corps of Signallers posing for the camera. Note the .303 SMLE rifle resting on the hedge. A signal cable can be seen running behind the soldiers on the hedge. (*WanPs-2133*)

(*Opposite below*) A photograph of a group of soldiers belonging to the Royal Canadian Corps of Signals. Note the sergeant who is armed with a pistol (holstered on his belt). A number of these men are wearing white armbands, reason unknown, but they may well be part of a unit acting as umpires during an exercise. Those not armed with a pistol are also wearing All-Arms pattern '37 double cartridge carrier ammunition pouches. These were normally issued to non-infantry units, e.g. mortar crews, armed with rifles, who did not need the ammunition carrying capacity of the larger basic pouch. The two tough looking soldiers on the bottom and rear rank on the right of the photograph are both wearing medal ribbons indicating that they served in the First World War. (*WanPs-2134*)

(*Above*) A photograph of two British soldiers, believed to have been taken in the Maidstone area. The corporal on the right is armed with a .303 pattern 1914 (P14) rifle. (*WanPs-2146*)

(*Opposite above*) Soldiers (probably Royal Engineers) being instructed by a corporal under instruction on a Gardner diesel engine. (*WanPs-2169*)

(*Opposite below*) New recruits at a Royal West Kent training depot, c.1940. (*WanPs-2327*)

An image showing what might be titled 'soldiers at play'. Why let a war spoil a good snowball fight! *(WanPs-2331)*

Mounted troops practising. Whilst the identity of the unit these men belong to is unknown, Territorial Yeomanry mounted cavalry regiments between the wars were re-roled as artillery. The two Yeomanry regiments that existed in Kent prior to amalgamation and conversion to an artillery unit were The Queen's Own West Kent Yeomanry and the The Royal East Kent Yeomanry. *(WanPs-2360)*

Soldiers live-firing Bren guns from the hip. The soldier in the middle is firing tracer ammunition which can be seen leaving the barrel of the gun, and is firing left handed. *(WanPs-2369)*

A group of soldiers of the Royal Army Service Corps. Where these men are heading is not known, but one soldier seated at the front right appears to have a tropical topee on the top of his pack. *(WanPs-2373)*

(*Above*) Soldiers in shirtsleeves, practising with a 3-inch mortar. (*WanPs-2453*)

(*Opposite above*) Soldiers photographed enjoying the proverbial cuppa in a Church Canteen at Folkestone. (*WanPs-2468*)

(*Opposite below*) A military parade taking place at an unknown location in Kent with the regimental mascot at the front. The mascot appears to be a Kashmir goat which is associated with Welsh Regiments (The Royal Welsh Fusiliers, The Royal Regiment of Wales, and the Royal Welsh Regiment). It is believed that the men on this parade are those of the Royal Welsh Fusiliers. The 53rd (Welsh) Infantry Division was based in Kent from 1941 to 1943. (*WanPs-2474*)

A military parade believed to be at Crescent Road, Tunbridge Wells. The unit being inspected is the 1st Battalion London Scottish. The London Scottish was a London based Territorial unit, part of 168 Brigade, 56 London Division, and known to have been based at Broome Park, near Barham at the end of April 1940. *(WanPs-2497)*

The pipe band of the London Scottish being inspected at Crescent Road (opposite assembly rooms), Tunbridge Wells. *(WanPs-0170)*

Chapter Five

Military Vehicles in Kent During World War Two

This chapter pertains to a broad selection from the photo archive and represents the various aspects of military vehicles that were photographed in Kent during the Second World War. They represent an interesting cross-section and include armoured vehicles, transport vehicles, motor-bikes and an assortment of other interesting examples. They demonstrate the variety of vehicles needed to support an Army. The development of military vehicles can be followed, with images of early Cruiser tanks, through to the much larger Churchill tank. The vehicles are largely of British design and manufacture, but also include Commonwealth and some lend-lease vehicles. The emphasis on British vehicles is most likely as a result of the lack of US units based in Kent, as they were largely based in the south-west of the country.

The crew of this Covenantor (Cruiser Mk V) tank is photographed changing a track, c.1942. *(WanPs-0220)*

Allied vehicles often come under criticism in relation to their design and their ability to resist attack. Whether this is fair or not, they certainly played a vital role in the defeat of the Nazi war machine. They are a testament to the men and women who built them and the men who fought in them and delivered the final overwhelming victory against the Axis forces throughout the world.

A Covenantor tank firing its 2-pdr gun on exercise, c.1942. (WanPs-2444)

A Crusader Mk III A15 (Cruiser Mk VI) tank with a 6-pdr gun on a training exercise, c.1942. The soldier seated on the front bulkhead is most likely a driving instructor communicating instructions to a trainee driver. (WanPs-0057)

Another view of the same Crusader tank. (WanPs-2484)

A Crusader Mk III tank on exercise 'somewhere in Kent'. *(WanPs-0192)*

A Royal Tank Regiment Matilda Mk III CS (close support) tank on manoeuvres in Kent, c.1942. The armament consists of a 3″ howitzer and a 7.92 BESA machine gun. *(WanPs-2492)*

(*Left*) Another view of the Royal Tank Regiment Matilda. (*WanPs-0232*)

(*Opposite page*) A Valentine Tank which has been named 'Dover' photographed partially camouflaged. The large funnel secured to the back of the chassis is for refuelling the vehicle. (*WanPs-0208*)

(*Below*) Valentine tanks of the 6th Armoured Division occupy a Kent village. (*WanPs-0215*)

(*Above*) The crew of a Valentine tank somewhere in Kent on exercise, c.1942. The crew are taking advantage of the halt and cooking something to eat. (*WanPs-0233*)

(*Opposite above*) A Valentine tank in action on exercise, c.1942. (*WanPs-2443*)

(*Opposite below*) A Mk II Churchill tank. This version of the Churchill tank featured a 2-pdr gun mounted in the turret as main armament along with a 7.92mm Besa machine gun. Another Besa machine gun was also mounted at the front of the vehicle to left of the driver position. (*WanPs-0193*)

A Churchill tank in the High Street at Headcorn, c.1942. The crew appear to be taking a break and having a cup of tea and something to eat whilst changing or repairing a track. (WanPs-2218)

The crew of this Churchill tank belonging to the Canadian 11th Armoured Regiment (The Ontario Regiment) are marking up notional exercise 'kills' on the turret. They appear to have done quite well! Life in a tank was a sometimes difficult and dirty business. As a result the crew of this Churchill tank T301030 are all dressed practically, if not particularly smartly! (WanPs-2477)

A Churchill tank photographed under a camouflage net at the pond in the village of Otford near Sevenoaks, c.1944. (WanPs-2493)

A Mk 2 Universal carrier on a training exercise. This photograph shows the excellent cross country capability of this small tracked carrier. (WanPs-0071)

(*Above*) A Universal Carrier. The soldier defending the roadblock is manning a Boys anti-tank rifle. To his left a Bren gun can also be seen. On the driver's left is a Bren gun. The roadblock seems rather unimpressive, and firing the Boys anti-tank rifle from a seated position is certainly not recommended due to its heavy recoil. (*WanPs-2491*)

(*Opposite above*) A Canadian Universal Carrier passes a Valentine tank from the 11th Armoured Division in the centre of Goudhurst, c.1942. (*WanPs-0196*)

(*Opposite below*) Troops and Universal Carriers from a Canadian Infantry Brigade outside The Bell Inn in the village of Frittenden, between Royal Tunbridge Wells and Ashford, c.1942. (*WanPs-2435*)

A Morris Commercial CDSW light AA 6 × 4 gun tractor photographed towing a 40mm Bofors AA gun of the 6th Armoured Division. (*WanPs-0195*)

A well camouflaged Ordnance QF 2-pdr Mk IX anti-tank gun on Carriage Mk I. (*WanPs-0209*)

A section of 18/25 QF (18lb gun barrel mounted on a 25lb gun carriage) guns on exercise. *(WanPs-0212)*

A rear view of the gun and detachment 18/25 QF gun. These guns are not actually firing live ammunition. From the markings on the ammunition box to the left of gun, it can be seen that they are actually firing blank ammunition. *(WanPs-0214)*

(*Left*) Royal Artillery soldiers manning a QF 2-pdr anti tank gun. (*WanPs-0213*)

(*Right*) A Norton army motorbike and rider. (*WanPs-0224*)

A Canadian artillery anti-tank unit moving through a Kent Village. Three Bedford MWD 15cwt 4 × 2 trucks are following a 4 × 4 Guy Ant Quad gun tractor, which is towing a French 75mm gun. The motorcycle on the right of the photograph belongs to the British 3rd Infantry Division. (*WanPs-0231*)

This photograph shows a group of despatch rider motorcyclists. *(WanPs-0341)*

A convoy photographed in the Kent countryside, with motorcycle outriders at the head of the column. *(WanPs-2437)*

A Royal Signals dispatch rider with a pigeon carrier back pack on a BSA M20 Motorcycle. *(WanPs-2481)*

A senior officer inspecting a GMC ACK-353 4 × 4 1.5 ton LHD truck, an ex-French contract vehicle used by British Army. The front hubs are designed to take dual wheels. Maidstone, c.1941. *(WanPs-0140)*

A Canadian Army Ford CMP No. 11 cab F60H 3-ton 6 × 4 truck followed by two Chevrolet CMP No. 12 cab C30 30cwt 4 × 4 trucks and an Albion 3-ton truck pass through Goudhurst. A Harley Davidson motorbike passes going in the opposite direction. (WanPs-0216)

A Royal Signals AEC 4 × 4 armoured command vehicle from the 8th Armoured Division. Big and comfortable, they were nicknamed Dorchesters after the luxury London hotel, c.1942. (WanPs-2431)

Chapter Six

VIP Visitors to Kent in Wartime

With its closeness to occupied Europe, the impact of the war on Kent was dramatic. 'Hellfire Corner'– the area nearest to occupied Europe and on the outskirts of London – was the county which directly suffered the greatest impact of the war and German attacks.

Its closeness to London also made it relatively easy for VIPs to visit. As a result, the county received visits to both the civilian population as well as to the armed forces stationed in Kent. Visitors included the Prime Minister Winston Churchill, King George VI and the Queen, The Duke of Kent (although he was killed in an air crash on 25 August 1942) and Princess Marina, Duchess of Kent. All would visit Kent on a number of occasions.

During the war royal visits were not subject to preliminary announcements, for security reasons. Because they visited unannounced, often with the shortest of notice, they were sometimes not greeted by thronging crowds.

Shortly after a devastating cross-Channel bombardment of Dover, it was suggested that the King and Queen visit, to encourage the inhabitants. They drove through the streets viewing the damage and the King suggested that they should call on a home which had been closely affected by the shelling. The mayor agreed and the King, wearing his customary naval uniform, alighted from the car with the Queen by his side. Their rap brought a teenaged girl to open the door. 'Is your mother home?' the King enquired, as he and Her Majesty stepped forward. 'No, she ain't', replied the girl, 'but she said, "if a sailor and a lady calls, you're to tell 'em they can 'ave the upstairs backroom for 5 shillings for an hour."'

The King visited East Kent again on 12 April 1940 to inspect military units. He had been forced to cut short another previously owing to a snowstorm. He had promised to visit again and was as good as his word when he returned again soon in April.

As a result of the customary lack of preliminary notice, when the King visited Dover Castle it only became apparent that he was in the area when the royal car was seen to arrive, and the Union Jack flying from the castle keep was replaced by the Royal standard, measuring 20ft × 10ft. Arriving at the castle at 12.25pm, after driving through the town he proceeded to inspect infantry battalions, a signal training battalion, and army classes who were seen at work at various stages of their training. He finished off the visit to the castle by inspecting a contingent of ATS. During the visit the King's progress was marked by enthusiastic cheers wherever he went.

After visiting the castle the King went on to inspect other units in the area which included an anti-aircraft battery, two more bodies of infantry, and field artillery units going through various phases of training. The King returned to Dover at the end of the visit and returned to London, travelling by special train from Dover Marine Station.

Both the King and Queen paid another visit to Dover and Folkestone in October 1944. The visit started at Dover where they inspected an honour guard formed by the Women's Royal Naval Service, The Women's Auxiliary Air Force, The Auxiliary Territorial Service and the National Fire Service. The people of Dover thronged the battered streets and welcomed the royal entourage. Whilst at Dover the King and Queen visited the underground cave shelters in Dover where the people were forced to take shelter during the German bombardments from across the Channel and from the air. From Dover the royal couple travelled to Folkestone where they were given another great welcome at the county cricket ground.

The Prime Minister Winston Churchill visited the county in the autumn of 1942, accompanied by the President of South Africa, Field Marshal Smuts, Mr Henry Morgenthau (Secretary of the US Treasury), and Mr Averell Harriman (President Franklin D. Roosevelt's special envoy to Europe). Arriving at Dover Priory station the party was greeted by the Mayor, Alderman J.R. Cairns, and senior military officers representing the Navy and the Army.

The announcement of their arrival had been communicated about an hour before to the townspeople by means of the loudspeakers used to give warning of immediate danger from enemy action – a method which enabled considerable numbers of people to congregate along the route from the station to the land at the rear of the police station where General Smuts and the Prime Minister were to inspect repre-sentatives of the civil defence services. The couple were cheered along the route as they passed by.

On this visit Churchill chose to dress in a dark coat and peaked hat accompanied with his proverbial cigar and stick. The Prime Minister stated that he was very happy to come down to Dover and to find that after three years of war the defence services were in good spirits. He felt sure that the spirit of Dover, this ancient port famous throughout the world, guardian of the white cliffs, was as high as it had ever been.

The Duke and Duchess of Kent also visited during the war, although the Duke was tragically killed when the Sunderland flying boat in which he was flying whilst heading to Iceland, where the Duke was to meet senior members of the US military, crashed into Eagle's Rock, near Dunbeath, Caithness. He was the only member of the royal family in recent times to have died on active service.

Prior to his death the Duke had visited Kent in September and December of 1940. On 5 September he visited the Royal Observer Corps post at Dover where its members kept an unbroken watch day and night. He stayed for a considerable time, was keenly interested in everything, and displayed quite a knowledge of observer work. He congratulated the crew on its great help to the Air Force and thanked the Head Observer for the privilege of being allowed to visit the nearest Observer Corps post to the enemy. In December 1940 he again visited Dover, this time to go to an ARP control centre. Afterwards the Duke visited some of the cave shelters and chatted to people who had taken refuge there, as there had actually been an air raid alert during his visit. The Duke also saw some of the considerable damage inflicted on the town.

The formal announcement of his death read: 'The Air Ministry deeply regrets to announce that Air Commodore His Royal Highness the Duke of Kent was killed on active service yesterday afternoon, when a Sunderland flying boat crashed in the North of Scotland. His Royal Highness, who was attached to the staff of the inspector-general of The Royal Air Force, was proceeding to Iceland on duty. All the crew of the flying boat lost their lives.' A subsequent message stated that the rear gunner had later been found alive. The Duke had a long association with the county of Kent. He met his future wife to be, Princess Marina, at Dover when she arrived in the county prior to their marriage in November 1934. He was also Colonel-in-Chief of the Royal West Kent Regiment.

On hearing of the tragic news of his death, the Mayor of Dover (Alderman J.R. Cairns) sent the following telegram to the Duchess of Kent: 'The Corporation and inhabitants of Dover have learned with profound regret of your irreparable loss, and tender their heartfelt and respectful sympathy in your great sorrow.' The Duchess's reply to this heartfelt message of sympathy read: 'Please convey to the town Council and the people of Dover my grateful thanks for their kind message, which has touched me deeply – Marina.'

After the Duke's death, Princess Marina continued to visit the county in her role as Commandant of the Women's Royal Naval Service (WRNS).

(*Above*) The original caption for this photo read, 'April 1940, the King and Queen brought cheer to troops when they visited east Kent. The King inspected defence preparations along the coast. Here he is seen at Shorncliffe, Folkestone.' (*WanPs-2160*)

(*Opposite above*) Another photograph showing the King's visit to Shorncliffe in April 1940. (*WanPs-2158*)

(*Opposite below*) King George VI and Queen Elizabeth during a visit to Kent. This photograph is taken at Folkestone cricket ground in October 1944. (*WanPs-0477*)

(*Above*) Prime Minister Winston Churchill during a visit to the 53rd (Welsh) Division on 20 November 1942. The photograph is taken at Mote Park, Maidstone. It is a classic study of Winston Churchill with his characteristic Homburg hat, cigar and walking stick. The Commander Home Forces, Lieutenant General Sir Bernard Paget GCB DSO MC, is pictured on the far right. On the far left, Winston Churchill's personal bodyguard Detective Inspector Walter Henry Thompson can also be seen. It was during this visit that Churchill was shown the new British Infantry Service rifle for the first time, the Lee-Enfield No. 4. (*WanPs-0009*)

(*Opposite above*) This photograph shows a mine clearing demonstration taking part during the Prime Minister's visit to the 53rd (Welsh) Division at Mote Park, Maidstone. Churchill and his party of senior officers seem to be enjoying a joke! (*WanPs-0194*)

(*Opposite below*) The last of the series of photographs showing Prime Minister Winston Churchill visiting the 53rd (Welsh) Division, Mote Park, Maidstone. The party can be seen here crossing a Folding Boat Equipment (FBE) Bridge. (*WanPs-2190*)

(*Left*) This photograph shows King George VI and Major-General Montgomery at XII Corps HQ at Broadwater Down, Tunbridge Wells on 13 June 1941. Montgomery had taken command of XII Corps in April 1941, and was responsible for the defence of Kent. During this period he instituted a regime of continuous training and insisted on high levels of physical fitness, for both officers and other ranks alike. He became known for being ruthless in sacking officers he considered would be unfit for command in action. (*WanPs-1104*)

(*Opposite page*) Princess Marina, Duchess of Kent, inspecting The Women's Royal Naval Service (WRNS) at HMS Pembroke, Chatham. Princess Marina was the Commandant of the Women's Royal Naval Service. (*WanPs-1159*)

(*Below*) The Duke of Kent with the Mayor of Canterbury, Alderman Charles Lefevre, inspecting the Auxiliary Fire Service at Watling Street car park, Canterbury in May 1941. The Duke of Kent was killed in an air crash in August 1942. (*WanPs-2384*)

Another photograph showing Princess Marina inspecting The WRNS at Chatham. HMS Pembroke was the Naval Barracks at Chatham, and was located next to Chatham Dockyard. (*WanPs-1160*)

Chapter Seven

The War at Sea

The Kent coastline is approximately 214 miles long. It incorporates a number of ports and harbours that have been used for commerce and military purposes for thousands of years. In the year 1050 a confederation known as the Cinque Ports was created which involved Hastings, Romney, Hythe, Dover and Sandwich assuming a special arrangement with the King whereby in return for the provision of ships and men for fifteen days free service a year to the Crown the town received privileges.

The Royal Navy has had dockyards in Kent at Chatham and Sheerness since the sixteenth and seventeenth centuries. Chatham Dockyard was established as a Royal dockyard by Elizabeth I in 1567. It became particularly important at this time owing to its strategic position on the River Medway. Its importance as a naval port declined due to the silting of the Medway making navigation difficult. As a result Chatham became a building yard rather than refitting base. In the 1860s the yard had a large building programme and St Mary's basin was constructed for the steam navy. HMS Pembroke, the Royal Naval Barracks at Chatham opened in 1903. The dockyard and naval base played a major part in supporting the Royal Navy until it was formally closed in 1984. The dockyard is now run as a museum by the Chatham Historic Dockyard Trust.

Sheerness Dockyard is situated at the mouth of the River Medway. The dockyard was founded in 1665, initially for storing and refitting ships. In 1720, a second dry dock was built and it became a ship construction yard. Between 1815 and 1826 it was completely rebuilt, and in 1854 a steam yard was established. It closed in 1957.

The Royal Navy connections with Kent form part of a long and proud naval tradition with the county.

Chatham dockyard became synonymous with the building of submarines, which began in 1907 and continued for over sixty years. The first was the coastal submarine C17 and the last was the Oberon class *Okanagan*, which was completed in 1968 for the Royal Canadian Navy. A total of fifty-seven submarines of twenty different classes were completed at Chatham.

Not only submarines were built at Chatham. Perhaps the Royal Navy's most famous ship of all, HMS *Victory*, was built there. Other ships, such as the cruisers HMS *Arethusa* and HMS *Euryalus*, which served during the Second World War, were also built at Chatham.

During the Second World War, the Royal Air Force also operated units at sea based in Kent to provide vital air-sea rescue services.

From 1918 to 1986 the Marine Branch of the Royal Air Force supplied waterborne support, rescue facilities, and services for the Royal Air Force throughout the world. Inaugurated as the Marine Craft Section, just eleven days after the Royal Air Force itself was founded, it initially provided back-up for the flying boats, but it also developed a rescue service which during and after the Second World War became the largest in the world. During the war years alone over 8,000 lives were saved by the crews of the high speed rescue launches who faced enemy action and all weathers to uphold their pledge of 'The Sea Shall Not Have Them'.

In addition to their routine duties in Air Sea Rescue, RAF marine craft operating from their bases at Sheerness and from the ferry dock at Dover, also participated in major amphibious operations such as the evacuation of Dunkirk in 1940, and Operation Jubilee at Dieppe in 1942.

RAF No. 27 Air-Sea Rescue Marine Craft Unit (ASRMCU) operated from the ferry dock at Dover. Launches of No. 27 ASRMCU came under enemy shell fire many times from German shore batteries while carrying out rescue operations within short distances of the enemy coast. They also frequently crossed dangerous minefields in order to reach ditched aircrews. During 1944, during the V1 blitz, the unit's launches were fitted with signal rockets, so that when they were operating near the enemy coast and saw flying bombs coming over, they could fire rockets as a warning to patrolling aircraft and to shore-based anti-aircraft batteries. As a result of this work the unit was credited with assisting with the destruction of four flying bombs. It was also credited with two enemy aircraft shot down in self-defence and one 'probable' on other operations. Among the many rescues of the unit were British, Allied and enemy airmen, and it also captured one enemy spy picked up from a canoe a few minutes after he had been dropped by an E-Boat. The Air Sea Rescue launches were under RAF Administration but were under naval orders when operating at sea.

An example of their particpation in amphibious operations took place during the Dieppe operation in August 1942. Among the fourteen high-speed RAF launches called out on 19 August 1942 during the Dieppe Raid (Operation Jubilee), in response to no less than forty-seven mayday calls, were the Dover based No. 27 ASRMCU launches HSLs 122, 123, 147 and 186. Two of the boats, HSL 122 and HSL 123 were lost on this operation. An official report submitted after the operation describes the events that took place:

> At about 16.35, four miles SE of the position, going north, 123 was attacked by two out of four FW 190s that appeared ahead. LAC Wilkins was wounded and Sergeant Smith slightly wounded. A 'Help' signal was sent. The planes did not return and course was maintained. Shortly afterwards the boat was challenged from the shore and the batteries opened fire, the shells falling astern. At 16.50

four FW 190s attacked from the port beam and course was altered towards them and no casualties resulted. A second 'Help' signal was sent. Course was altered to NW to try and shake off the planes, which again disappeared, and to contact 122 for mutual aid and support. 122 when sighted, was being bombed by a Heinkel and when closed at 17.15 was found to have been badly damaged by cannon and machine-gun fire, and with only five men left alive. These were being transferred when six or eight FW 190s appeared and attacked from the port beam, four serious casualties being sustained. A signal 'Urgent Help 182 Dungeness 23' was sent. The boats then became separated. In view of the fact that not a single British fighter had provided cover or was even sighted from the time the English coast was left, and that we had been informed that none could be expected, it was considered that absolutely no possibility remained of making the twenty-five miles to our coast against the concerted attacks in operation. The boat [122] was therefore abandoned at 17.20. While the survivors were in the water both boats were attacked for about half an hour and set completely on fire … HSL 177, five to six miles distant, apparently saw smoke and having contacted RML 513 and two Spitfires, proceeded and performed a plucky and skilful rescue at about 18.00, the FW 190s making off on their approach …'

One of those on board HSL 122 who demonstrated the devotion to duty and contempt for danger so often shown by the crews of RAF air-sea rescue launches, was Leading Aircraftsman Albert Dargue. His actions on the 19 August resulted in the award of a British Empire Medal (the BEM can be awarded for gallantry, but a degree less than that required to earn the George Medal). His award citation reads:

Leading Aircraftman Dargue was Nursing Orderly on a High Speed Launch during the combined operations on 19 August 1942. In spite of wounds, he endeavoured to carry out first-aid to the wounded until he was picked up in a seriously wounded condition. The courage and valuable services rendered by Leading Aircraftman Dargue are typical of the high qualities displayed by the nursing orderlies, who have carried out hazardous operations in High Speed Launches which play an essential part in Air Sea Rescue.

Dargue was plucked from the water by Flight Lieutenant D.R. 'Don' Morrison DFC DFM No. 401 (RCAF) Squadron, himself having been picked up by HSL 177 after being downed earlier that day.

Air Commodore Graham Pitchfork's *Shot Down and in the Drink, RAF and Commonwealth Aircrews Saved from the Sea 1939–45* describes the events of Albert Dargue's rescue:

Morrison noticed a semi-conscious seaman drifting away. He immediately dived into the sea and burning oil to reach the badly injured man, bringing him alongside the launch where he was recovered on board. He was Leading Aircraftman

Albert Dargue, the medical orderly of HSL 122, which had been attacked and set on fire by German fighters. Despite being badly hurt himself, Dargue tended the seriously wounded until HSL 123 pulled alongside. Only four men were left alive and Dargue dragged the other three survivors on deck, but just as they were about to be transferred, HSL 123 also came under attack and was severely damaged. As the launch caught fire, the master gave the order to abandon ship. Dargue inflated the Mae Wests of the three injured men and pushed them overboard before he jumped. Exhausted and weak from his wound, he could do little to help himself until Morrison rescued him.'

Once HSL 177 had picked up the fourteen survivors the master headed for New-haven at full speed, where the wounded were quickly evacuated to hospital. Morrison returned to his squadron and was soon back on duty.

Following the Dieppe operation there were a number of gallantry awards for the men of the RAF's high speed launches, including an MBE to Conway and a BEM to the brave LAC Albert Dargue.

Morrison wrote a detailed report of his experiences but made no mention of his own courageous part. He was loud in his praise for the men who manned the RAF rescue launches and concluded his report: 'There can be no question as to the bravery of these men of the Air Sea Rescue Service who were often working within sight of the French coast. For myself, I would rather meet a FW 190 head-on in my Spitfire than meet one from a rescue launch.'

Praise indeed from a brave pilot. Don Morrison was again shot down in December 1943. Posted as missing he was feared killed. He had actually been taken prisoner but had been seriously wounded (his left leg was amputated above the knee by German doctors). He was eventually repatriated in November 1943.

(*Opposite page*) An RAF air-sea rescue launch off the coast of Kent, c.1943. (*WanPs-0172*)

(*Above*) The view looking over the bow of an air-sea rescue launch. The typical red and white chequerboard markings of an ASR launch can be made out in this photograph. Originally the decks and superstructure of ASR launches were painted yellow to make the launches as conspicuous as possible from the air, but the frequency of German air attacks on the launches resulted in the substitution of grey paint. (*WanPs-0254*)

(*Opposite above*) A gunner on RAF air-sea rescue launch manning twin .303 Vickers K machine guns. (*WanPs-0287*)

(*Opposite above*) An RAF Air Sea Rescue Launch at sea. The difficulty of spotting downed aircrew is illustrated by this photograph – the sea is a very big place and spotting even a boat the size of an ASR launch can be difficult in the best of sea conditions. (*WanPs-0256*)

(*Above*) An armed trawler manned by army personnel. The gun is a .303 Hotchkiss machine gun. These First World War vintage machine guns were considered obsolete when the Second World War broke out, but the shortage of weapons forced them to be used as air defence weapons on ships pressed into service. The soldier on the far left is wearing the badge of the 77th Infantry Division. This division was formed from the Devon and Cornwall Division on 1 December 1941. It remained in the United Kingdom throughout the war, was converted into a reserve formation in December 1942, and disbanded in September 1944. (*WanPs-0202*)

(*Opposite above*) A naval party marching north near Southbourough Common the A26 London Road, Southborough, c.1943. (*WanPs-2335*)

(*Opposite below*) Royal Marines on parade at the Marine Barracks Chatham c.1941. The Royal Marines were based at Chatham for over 200 years. From 1775 until 1950 the Chatham Division of Royal Marines occupied barracks on a site adjacent to the southern end of the Dockyard. The barracks were demolished in the 1950s. (*WanPs-2385*)

(*Above*) HMS *Orion* photographed at Chatham Dockyard. Built at Devonport Dockyard, *Orion* took part in the bombardment of Bardia, and the Battle of Calabria in July 1940. In 1941 *Orion* took part in the Battle of Cape Matapan and the evacuation of Crete, where she was bombed and badly damaged. Subsequently, after being repaired, she took part in convoy escort duties, the invasion of Sicily, and the Normandy Landings in June 1944. She was scrapped by Arnott Young at Dalmuir, in Scotland in 1949. (*WanPs-2838*)

(*Opposite top*) This photograph shows HMS *Kent*, believed to have been taken after her refit at Chatham in 1938. HMS *Kent* was a County-class heavy cruiser and was constructed at Chatham. During 1940 she was assigned to troop convoy escort duties in the Indian Ocean, then transferred to the Mediterranean in mid-1940, where she was torpedoed shortly after arriving. The ship was under repair for a year and was then assigned to Home Fleet where she escorted convoys to and from North Russia. In mid-1944 *Kent* escorted British aircraft carriers as their aircraft made attacks on German shipping and airfields in Norway. This ship, as might be expected, has a close association with the county of Kent. Her badge was the White Horse of Kent on a Field Red and her motto: Invicta – unconquered. (*WanPs-2842*)

(*Opposite middle*) HMS *Kent* at Chatham, photographed before the war in 1937. (*WanPs-2841*)

(*Opposite bottom*) This photograph is another fine study of a Royal Navy Warship, believed to be either HMS *Achilles* or HMS *Orion* leaving Chatham Dockyard. (*WanPs-2845*)

HMS *Dido* photographed at Chatham Dockyard in 1945. HMS *Dido* was a Dido class light cruiser. She was built by Cammell Laird at Birkenhead, UK and was launched on 18 July 1939. She was adopted by the civil community of Bolton, Lancashire. Her battle honours are listed: CRETE 1941 – SIRTE 1942 – MEDITERRANEAN 1942–44 – MALTA CONVOYS 1942 – SICILY 1943 – SALERNO 1943 – AEGEAN 1943 – ANZIO 1944 – SOUTH FRANCE 1944 – ARCTIC 1944. She returned to Chatham for a refit in October 1945. On completion in 1947, owing to economic constraints on defence expenditure and manning difficulties, the ship was placed in reserve. She never re-commissioned and was eventually scrapped in 1956 at Barrow-in-Furness. (*WanPs-2850*)

Chapter Eight

Women at War in Kent

The Auxiliary Territorial Service

The Auxiliary Territorial Service (ATS) came into being on 9 September 1938. It was initially organised on a regional basis in the same way as the Territorial Army. It incorporated members of the First Aid Nursing Yeomanry (FANY), the earliest women's voluntary corps, which had served with distinction in the First World War. The first women who joined the ATS had no uniform and received only an armband with the initials 'A.T.S.' which they put over the sleeve of their civilian clothing. They received little training and worked mainly on such duties as cooks, clerks and storekeepers. In April 1941, the members of the ATS were given full military status. In December 1941 the government passed the National Service Act, which allowed the conscription of women into war work or the armed forces. Women could choose to join the ATS or its naval or air force equivalents, the WRNS and the WAAF. After the initial influx of volunteers a system of basic training was established lasting six weeks. New recruits were issued with their uniform and asked to carry out trade tests to establish which area they should go into. Experience in civilian life was usually taken into account; for example, if a woman had been a shorthand typist she would almost certainly be assigned clerical duties. During the course of the war the range of duties undertaken by the ATS expanded and women worked as telephonists, drivers, mechanics, mess orderlies, butchers, bakers, postal workers, ammunition inspectors and military police. The expanding role of the ATS in Kent was made apparent in a local newspaper report in May 1942:

> ATS Women are to be trained at civilian garages in order to speed up the output of qualified driver mechanics. The first batch of 45 ATS trainees are now taking a six weeks course. They are all recent recruits, who have already done a driving course at an ATS MT Training Centre.

An appeal was also issued for recruits in May 1942:

> Several hundred women of exceptional intelligence and proved organising ability are wanted at once to train as ATS cooks.

Whilst some members of the ATS may have been engaged in more traditional female roles, by 1944 some were employed in trades usually associated with men. The *Dover Herald* reported on 25 August 1944:

> Armoured fighting vehicles, including tanks, armoured cars and Bren gun carriers, are now being repaired and adjusted by the A.T.S. before being sent to battle areas. It is a tough job, and before A.T.S. do it they train for a stiff six months training course, becoming skilled vehicle mechanics able to tackle such work as, stripping down tank engines, assembling Bren gun carriers and re-building armoured cars. Despite the constant clang of the R.E.M.E. workshops where they are employed and the dirt and grease connected with their work these A.T.S. consider themselves fortunate to be doing a 'man-sized' job.

The report went on to cite the personal story of Private Bessie Hayes of Lyndale House, Ashley near Dover who while training for her work first met her husband Roy Topley of Melton Mowbray who was also learning to become a welder.

The work of the ATS was not limited to work providing support services to the Army. In Kent they worked as plotters for the channel guns. It was members of the ATS who plotted the course of the *Scharnhorst*, *Gneisenau* and *Prinz Eugen* during their Channel dash in February 1942. The plotters worked in 24-hour shifts, manning the front line plotting rooms on the South Coast. Their job was to chart the course of every Allied or enemy ship which passed our shores within their area.

In one plotting room the ATS had a collection of trophies: splinters or shells fired in action and sent by a coast regiment, as recognition of the behind the scenes work performed by ATS which enabled them to engage the enemy. One exhibit of which the ATS plotters were immensely proud was the tracing of the SS *Munsterland* which they plotted throughout its two hour run before being finally sunk by coast artillery of the Wanstone and South Foreland batteries. The *Munsterland* was a German blockade-runner which had sailed from Japan with a cargo vital for Germany's armaments industry. The sinking of this ship was a significant blow to German industry.

Whilst much of the work performed by the ATS was in a supporting role, some members lost their lives as a result of the sometimes hazardous duties they had to perform. One of those that paid the ultimate price was 42-year-old Corporal Lilian Bidgood of Loose, near Maidstone. She was crushed to death by the wheels of a 50 ft tank transporter and trailer at a southern base Army Reception Park. She is commemorated today at the Brookwood Military Cemetery in Surrey.

The Women's Land Army

The Women's Land Army was formed in 1939. It called for volunteers to take the place of thousands of young male farm workers who had gone off to fight in the war.

With the country at war and all able-bodied men needed to fight, there was a shortage of labour to work on farms and in other jobs on the land. At the same time it was becoming increasingly difficult to get food imported from abroad, so more land needed to be farmed to provide home-grown food. The Women's Land Army provided much of the labour force to work this land.

The advertising slogan read, 'For a healthy, happy job join The Women's Land Army'. In reality, the work was hard and dirty and the hours were long. Some of the girls received training before they were sent to farms; the farmers themselves trained others.

The Timber Corps was set up in 1942 to teach women to make pit props, necessary for working in mines. By 1944 the WLA had over 80,000 members. It lasted until its official disbandment on 21 October 1949.

Life in Kent for the Women's Land Army was certainly eventful. In September 1942, at Westcourt Farm, Shepherdswell, a village between Canterbury and Dover, the farmer Mr James Weir on a Monday afternoon was driving some heifers, with a bull, into a field when the bull attacked him and he fell unconscious. Without hesitation, 26-year-old Miss Laura Jennings, a member of the Women's Land Army, attacked the offending animal but was injured and thrown to the ground. She got up and continued to attempt to drive off the bull, which was afterwards successfully secured by other workers after it had been attacked by Mr Weir's collie dog. Both Mr Weir and Miss Jennings were taken to Canterbury hospital as a result of the attack. Originally from Huddersfield, Miss Jennings had only been at the farm for six weeks!

Working for the Women's Land Army in Kent also included other hazards, such as fires – some provided courtesy of the Luftwaffe.

A local newspaper report describes an event that took place in October 1942:

The girls and workmen at a farm near the S.E. Coast were machine gunned by a German raider last week. 'I was on the horse' said Theodora Marsh, 'when I saw a big plane very low, just seeming to skim the stacks. The noise was terrible, but my horse was really good and stood still. Of course we were scared but we soon got over it.' 'This is our hot field' said another girl. 'We've had missiles, fire, and now this Jerry. He must have missed the bus because the harvest is in.'

There are some of the girls who helped put out a fire in the barley a few weeks back and worked hard until the fire service arrived. They are indeed plucky girls, there is not much cover in the field but on they go with their work.

The report named the 'plucky' girls to give them a little limelight. Their names were recorded as: Theodora Marsh, Doreen Watts, Edith Beer and Ruth Fassams.

(*Above*) A member of the ATS tending some plants in a sea mine which is being used as a flower garden. This photograph is believed to have been taken at an ordnance store located at Appledore Road, Tenterden, c.1943. (*WanPs-2267*)

(*Opposite above*) Members of the ATS next to an American Chevrolet 1940-model panel van. The photograph was taken at Somerfield Terrace, London Road, Maidstone. (*WanPs-0079*)

(*Opposite below*) This photograph shows ATS female motor mechanics, being instructed on a Wolseley Saloon staff car. (*WanPs-0173*)

(*Above*) Land Army girls taking a break at a farm somewhere in Kent. (*WanPs-0041*)

(*Opposite page*) A photograph of a cheery ATS girl 'spud bashing', *c*.1941. (*WanPs-0242*)

(*Below*) Land Army girls photographed on parade in Tunbridge Wells, *c*.1943. (*WanPs-0324*)

(*Above*) Ambulance girls photographed on 28 October 1939. Marked on the steel helmet of the woman on the left, the FAP stands for first aid post. The lady on the far right also has an armband marked the same. (*WanPs-0112*)

(*Opposite page*) Three girls photographed lighting up a cigarette in the street, Kent, c.1940. (*WanPs-0159*)

(*Below*) Members of the Women's Auxiliary Police Corps on duty, c.1943. At the outbreak of the Second World War the Women's Auxiliary Police Corps was formed. WAPC duties consisted of giving assistance to the regular police, and included the driving and maintenance of motors and the repair of other equipment as well as clerical work and acting as telephone operators. In London and other cities there were also women beat patrols. At its peak in June 1943, 7,300 women were serving with the police. (*WanPs-0184*)

(*Above*) Girls of the Women's Junior Air Corps being instructed in aircraft identification. This photograph is believed to have been taken in Gravesend. The instructor is pointing to an identification silhouette of a Fairey Fulmar British carrier-borne fighter aircraft that served with the Fleet Air Arm (FAA) during the Second World War. (*WanPs-0218*)

(*Opposite above*) Members of the Women's Auxiliary Air Force (WAAF) parading during a Wings for Victory parade in Guildhall St, Canterbury, c.1942. (*WanPs-0226*)

(*Opposite below*) Female railway maintenance staff at Tunbridge Wells Station. During the Second World War women performed many roles on the railways. They were luggage porters, railway station announcers, booking clerks, ticket inspectors, welders, lathe operators and blacksmiths. They were also involved in manufacturing telegraph poles, manufacturing concrete railway sleepers, ticket printing, painting railway bridges, and crane operation – in fact many of the roles usually performed in peacetime by men. This vital work freed up hundreds of men for service in the Navy, the Army and the Air Force. (*WanPs-2458*)

Chapter Nine

D-Day and Kent

Kent would play an important part in D-Day. Operations to support the landings were carried out from here; part of the vital Pipeline Under the Ocean (PLUTO) was hosted from Dungeness; support for the Mulberry harbours was provided from the coast of Kent; and part of the vital deception plan intended to fool the Germans that the landing would be carried out in the Calais region, were amongst contributions made to the greater D-Day plans.

The deception plan codenamed Operation Fortitude was intended to draw the Germans' attention away from the true location of the D-Day landings by simulating large forces poised to land elsewhere. Hitler was convinced that the Allies would land in either Norway or northern France, or both, and consequently kept large forces in those areas to combat this threat. To encourage those beliefs, a deception plan was created and codenamed Fortitude (North) and Fortitude (South) which simulated large military formations in Scotland, North East England, and in the South East of England. The phantom force in the south-east was named the First United States Army Group (FUSAG) and its existence was created by the use of intense radio traffic between imaginary formations, the use of double agents and turned spies sending back false reports, 'innocent' news reports and security 'lapses' adding weight to reports, the use of dummy landing craft, vehicles and tanks, and the complete denial of the airspace of the South East of England to enemy reconnaissance aircraft.

Amongst the units based in Kent before, during and after D-Day were a number of American units. One of these, the United States Army 643rd Port Company, manned largely by African American troops, arrived in the area to support operations after D-Day, towards the end of the war. Initially based in Wales, the unit's history provides an insight into the impression made on the soldiers as a result of their stay in Kent:

> We loaded our gear and selves into trucks for the Newport Railway Station. The station platform was crowded with our Welsh friends who came to say good-bye. Where we were going was anybody's guess. Those in the know wouldn't tell as per usual, 'Security you know'! We headed west toward London, then sidetracked. All of that afternoon we rode through the lush green meadows of rural Wales and England. About six bells our train skirted a very large body of

sky blue water. And then we saw them! Yes! Unmistakably the Great White Chalk Cliffs . . . no mistaking it, this is Dover on the English Channel. We'd always wanted to visit this place and here at last we were! About half an hour later our journey ended at Deal, a very picturesque resort town about seven miles from Dover. After debarkation was completed we stood around awhile doing nothing. Lt Saltzman, who had preceded us in the advance party, showed up after a while and we started on a short walk (it turned out to be four miles) to our new camp. We were impressed by the beautiful homes and quiet dignity of the villages of Deal and Walmer, through which we marched towards our new camp. The neat velvety lawns, which are so typical of all England, were quite in evidence. We thought that this was the most beautiful scenery that we had seen. Dover, Deal and Walmer are located in Kent, one of England's most beautiful shires or counties. We have just gotten our first glimpse of the Channel since being on terra-firma. It was a fleeting glance past the cylindrical Dover Castle which we passed 'on the go'. Several British Wrens and ATS girls waved at us. Passing Royal Marines gave the 'V' sign. People in the pubs along the route invited us in for a drink during 'breaks'. Of course we had to refuse, but we promised to join them later. Well at last we were there. We had been warned not to expect the 'ideal' camp. Forewarned was forearmed and we had, as per usual, our old reliable pup tents in our field packs. Our new campsite had a few semi-dilapidated buildings which would not accommodate all of the men and so we pitched tents.

Our new camp site is situated on a knoll overlooking 'Bomb Alley'. The German Bombers used to fly low across here on their bomb run to London. After a supper of rations we bedded down and snoozed until morning. Another day, another hard earned dollar. The doors of our tents were on the west permitting us to look straight across Bomb Alley towards the English Channel about a mile and half away. The chilly Kentish morning air stimulated our appetites and we looked across the way to see what 'les cousiniers' were doing. We were surprised to find that they had set up the field ranges. The smell of crisp bacon filled the air and we went all out for chow. We've attended orientation where we've been informed that we're the only American Troops on this side of London, some eighty miles distant. We learned that there have never been many Yank troops around and so had to be on our P's and Q's.

The men of the 643rd Port Company had been sent to Kent to assist with the salvage of an American Liberty ship, the SS *Horace Binney*, that had struck a mine and been towed back to England and beached on a sand bar. The work was dirty, disagreeable and not without danger. The holds were littered with waste and filled with cargo and oil. The unit history goes on to further describe their stay in Kent:

Those of us who chose to explore followed our noses down Bomb Alley as straight as the crow flies. We wanted to see what was 'over that hill' besides the Channel. We came upon the beautiful little village of Lansdowne. The haze lifted and we could see Calais about twenty miles across the Channel. A fleet of LCTs were moving in that direction from Dover farther up the beach. We noticed that most of the picture-book inns, cottages and pubs were just camouflaged gun positions. Only a few weeks before, the big guns talked back at each other from both sides. Barbed wire and steel obstructions were still on the beach. Part of the beach is still mined and we were particular to stay clear of the area marked. We could see part of the great oil storage tanks submerged in the earth with which the British had intended to transfer the channel literally into a sea of fire in the event of a German attempt at invasion. We collected a few sea shells and hurried back towards camp.

Operations commenced. The job, dirty and difficult, certainly taxed the energy and ingenuity of all concerned. We broke camp and on the morning of July 2, 1945 we entrained at Dover for Cardiff. We said, 'so long mates' to the Royal Marines at their barracks in Deal. We shall never forget their hospitality. Of the citizens of nearby Deal, Dover and Walmer, too much cannot be said. We shall simply say that we love them and let that suffice. The lights have now come on all over the world again.

This is the 'tomorrow when the world is free'. We hope that the bluebirds have taken the cue and are again winging their way over the White Cliffs. They couldn't have chosen a more hospitable or beautiful locale.

Pipeline Under The Ocean (PLUTO)

Planners knew that the future invasion of Europe would be the largest amphibious landing in history and without adequate and reliable supplies of petrol any advance would at best slow down and at worst grind to a halt. A loss of momentum could jeopardise the whole operation as German forces would have time to regroup and counter-attack. Conventional tankers and 'ship to shore' pipelines were in danger of cluttering up the beaches, obstructing the movement of men, armaments and materials and, in all circumstances, were subject to disruption by weather and sea conditions, and they were easy targets for the Luftwaffe. The idea of a pipeline under the Channel was an innovative solution.

Work on developing this idea began as early as 1942. Constructing flexible yet pressure-resistant pipes and leak-free couplings was a difficult and slow process. In addition, it was realised that the fuel would need to be stored in the south of England in the preparation stages for the invasion, with the possibility of the storage points becoming targets for the Luftwaffe. Consequently it was decided that an integrated network of pipelines would be needed, bringing the fuel from oil terminals and the like to safer areas of the United Kingdom, mainly Liverpool and Bristol, down to Dungeness and the Isle of Wight and from there over the Channel to Cherbourg and Calais.

In a very short time a continuous flow of fuel was up and running. It is estimated that between August 1944 and May 1945 PLUTO delivered over 172 million gallons to France. As the Allies moved inland, the pipeline was transferred from the Isle of Wight to Dungeness in Kent to shorten the supply route. PLUTO was the world's first undersea oil pipeline and made a major contribution, not only to the Allied war effort, but also to subsequent pipeline development.

Pipe Line Under The Ocean (PLUTO) control valves Dungeness, c.1945. *(WanPs-0001)*

A 'Conundrum' aground at Greatstone, c.1945. Following successful trials with a large prototype in early 1944, five of these giant floating pipeline drums, whose name was often shortened to 'conuns', were commissioned to a modified design. The new drums, with a 30ft diameter, were fabricated in Scunthorpe, erected in Tilbury Docks and launched into the Thames. Each of the conuns weighed in at 250 tons and had a combined capacity to carry up to seventy nautical miles of 3-inch diameter pipe, codenamed HAMEL pipe, that could be automatically welded together. (WanPs-0005)

American Airmen in Kent

One of the US Army Air Force units based in Kent on the run up to D-Day and after was the 363rd Fighter Group, which was located approximately one mile northeast of Staplehurst, about thirty-eight miles southeast of London. The airfield at Staplehurst had been opened in 1943, and was a prototype Advanced Landing Ground (ALG) type construction, built to the same design as those that were built in

Beach defences with the beached Conundrum at Greatstone in the background. *(WanPs-0006)*

and around the Normandy beachhead after D-Day. It was used by squadrons of the Royal Canadian Air Force and the United States Army Air Forces. The Ninth Air Force part of the USAAF utilised several temporary Advanced Landing Grounds along the channel coast prior to D-Day to provide tactical air support for the ground forces landing in Normandy. As such, the ALG at Staplehurst was utilised by the USAAF 363rd Fighter Group who moved there from RAF Rivenhall in Essex on 14 April 1944. Known officially as USAAF Station AAF-413, three squadrons (the 380th Fighter Squadron, the 381st Fighter Squadron, and the 382nd Fighter Squadron) equipped with North American P-51B fighter aircraft flew operations in preparation and then support of the Allied invasion of France. The group escorted bombers and fighter-bombers to targets in France, Germany, and the Low Countries, and strafed and dive-bombed trains, marshalling yards, bridges, vehicles, airfields, troops, gun positions, and other targets on the Continent. The 363rd supported the D-Day invasion of Normandy in June 1944 by escorting troop carriers and gliders and by attacking enemy positions near the front lines, and moved to the Continent at the end of June to take part in the Allied drive to the German border. The Group's operations resulted in a total of nineteen confirmed victories. However, a similar number of Mustangs were lost, albeit mostly to ground fire. On 30 June, the 363rd was alerted for movement to the Continent, its new base being the airfield at Maupertus (ALG A-15), near Cherbourg. The airfield at Staplehurst closed in September 1944.

One of the Group's operations, made while based at Staplehurst, is graphically described in the first-hand account of one of the pilots Lt Charles F. Stuart Jr, a P-51 pilot with the 381st Fighter Squadron. The event took place on 24 May 1944, returning to England after an escort mission to Berlin:

We were down on the deck, looking for targets of opportunity to strafe (anything that looks like it needs shooting at). If you look at the back of your right hand, your first finger would be a fellow named Shea, the next would be Schmidt, and the third finger would be this new replacement pilot Kennedy, I was on the far right. We had passed over some trees and then all of a sudden there was a German airfield right in front of us. The darn thing was sort of pear-shaped. Shea was way over on the left side. He was nearly a quarter of a mile from me, we were spread well out. Schmidt was in there and he kept calling this new pilot (Kennedy) to 'get off my wing'. The guy was flying right on his wing, close formation, just a few feet off the ground. I mean, it's suicide to fly like that; you need to spread out so you have a little manoeuvring room. I hit the field at the narrow end – the little end of the pear – and when I saw the thing there was a flak tower right square in my gunsight. They didn't even see me coming. I recall it had three or four 20mms on it, maybe ten men manning the thing, and they were raring back and shooting like the devil at Schmidt and that wingman out in the middle of the airfield. Shea was a little bit out of their range. I am not sure if they actually hit the new man, or whether he got scared, but he flipped over to the left & into Schmidt. The two of them went across that German airfield in one great big hellish ball of flame. A split second later, I hit my trigger and cleaned that platform out like a bowling ball knocks a strike down the alley. I think I knocked every darn one of them off the platform, but just a hair too late. That was about enough for Shea & I that day. We both revved back on the stick and got up to 15,000 or 20,000 feet. Without a word between us we closed back in, a few yards or so apart, flying abreast. Finally, Shea comes in and says, 'Did you see what I saw?' I said 'Yes, I saw what you saw, too.' As well as I can remember, we didn't say anything else until we got back to England. [Personal account taken from: http://www.warbirdinformationexchange.org/phpBB3/viewtopic.php?p=510886]

During operations from England, the group was credited with forty-one victories but lost forty-three of its own aircraft in the process.

Two memorials have been erected that commemorate the airfield's part in the Normandy Landings. One is dedicated to the Canadian and American pilots and their ground crews stationed at Chickenden Farm and Spills Hill Farm, Staplehurst. The second, unveiled on 6 June 2010, is dedicated to the American airmen who lost their lives flying from Staplehurst during the period 14 April 1944 to 4 July 1944.

An American military policeman and an American colonel at the 363rd Fighter Group airfield at Chickenden Farm, Staplehurst. (WanPs-2060)

(*Above*) This photograph shows people enjoying a dance for American servicemen held at Maidstone. (*WanPs-2378*)

(*Opposite page*) Members of the American 363rd fighter group at the Advanced Landing Ground, Chickenden Farm, Staplehurst. (*WanPs-2059*)

(*Below*) A US army survey unit photographed at Meopham. (*WanPs-2246*)

On the run-up to D-Day, the country roads were lined with equipment dumps. This photograph was taken 'somewhere in Kent' and shows an ammunition dump located by the roadside. *(WanPs-2214)*

An inevitable consequence of the successful invasion of France was the capture of thousands of German prisoners of war. Many of these POWs were employed in work around the countryside. These prisoners, photographed in Kent, are taking a break from the work they are carrying out. *(WanPs-0084)*

Chapter Ten

The End of the War

The end of the war in Europe came on 8 May 1945 – VE Day. The World War finally ended on 15 August with the surrender of Japan on VJ Day. For the generation that the war directly affected, the end was met with a mix of emotions. It had been a long war and there had been both triumph and tragedy for many of the people of Kent.

The effects of the Second World War will continue to be felt for many years to come. Today unexploded bombs and munitions continue to surface, and concrete anti-invasion defences still stand as mute reminders of the past. Whilst much redevelopment has occurred since the war, and the effects of intensive farming have changed much of the landscape, it is still possible to see many tangible reminders of the Second World War.

For many people, the war had been an appalling time, a time of fear, deprivation and loss. For some it had provided the ultimate challenge, with bonds of close comradeship forged that would never be forgotten.

Many celebrations were held throughout the county. On 11 May 1945, the *Dover and East Kent Express* described some of the events that took place in Dover and were typical of events throughout England:

> Tuesday May 8th will live for ever in history and in the minds of those who lived through the most terrible war the world has known. The war against Germany had lasted 5 years, 8 months and 5 days, when on Tuesday, Victory in Europe was celebrated. Dover in common with all other cities, towns and villages in this and other Allied countries, gave expression to joy and thanksgiving.
>
> Monday was a day of suspense with rumour following rumour. Every news was listened to from the first in the morning, and each time the announcement was that any hour the Prime Minister was expected to make his statement signalling the end of organised German resistance. Then after a statement at 6.00pm on the B.B.C. that the announcement was not expected until Tuesday, at 7.40pm, the broadcast was broken into to announce VE-Day holiday on Tuesday and Wednesday, with Mr Churchill's broadcast at 3.00pm on Tuesday.
>
> Dover was awake early on Tuesday morning. Overnight, flags decorated houses and shops, and soon others were being added in haste. The atmosphere

grew steadily during the morning until 3 o'clock in the afternoon, when the loud speakers – grim reminders of Dover's bitter ordeal from German shells – relayed the Prime Ministers declaration: 'Yesterday at 2.41am at headquarters, General Jodl, the representative of the German High Command and of Grand Admiral Donitz, the designated head of the German State, signed the act of unconditional surrender of all German land, sea and air forces in Europe.'

Winston Churchill's statement went on to detail how the surrender had taken place and he also included a resumé of the war. He went on to conclude:

> We may allow ourselves a brief period of rejoicing but let us not forget for a moment the toil and efforts that lie ahead. Japan, with all her treachery and greed, remains unsubdued. The injury she has influenced on Great Britain, the United States and other countries and her detestable cruelties, call for justice and retribution. We must now devote our strength and resources to the completion of our task, both at home and abroad. Advance Britannia. Long live the cause of freedom. God save the King.

At the end of the Prime Minister's statement, ships in the harbour greeted the declaration by sounding their sirens, creating a deafening noise. In the town, the streets were jammed and good-humouredly the police jostled amongst the crowds, trying to make room for traffic. Buses were decked in flags and from the windows people waved Union Jacks. American jeeps weaved through the crowds with their human cargo, cheering as they went. The crowds danced and sang for hours on end.
Later the King broadcast to the nation:

> To-day we give thanks to Almighty God for a great deliverance. Speaking from our Empire's oldest capital city, war-battered but never for one moment daunted or dismayed – speaking from London, I ask you to join with me in that act of thanksgiving. Germany, the enemy who drove all Europe into war, has finally been overcome.

The King's speech continued, acknowledging the job still to do in the continuing war against Japan, and also the job now required to repair the ravages of war. He continued:

> Let us turn our thoughts on this day of just triumph and sorrow, and then take up our work again, resolved as a people to do nothing unworthy of those who died for us and to make the world such a world as they would have desired, for their children and for ours.

A legacy that all of us should remember today, the debt we owe to those died and the many that went to war and who did not return.

At 0815 on the morning of 6 August 1945, the crew of B-29 44-86292 'Enola Gay', dropped a single atomic bomb which exploded over its target, the city of Hiroshima.

On the 9 May, B-29 44-27297 'Bockscar', dropped a second atomic bomb which exploded above Nagasaki at 11:02 local time.

Six days later the Japanese signed the formal instrument of surrender proclaiming the unconditional surrender to the Allied Powers of the Japanese Imperial General Headquarters and of all Japanese Armed Forces and all Armed Forces.

The war had finally ended.

A typical street party taking place on VE day 1945 in Kent. (WanPs-0239)

(*Above*) A VE day party at Nursery Road, High Brooms, Royal Tunbridge Wells, 6 June 1945. (*WanPs-2237*)

(*Opposite above*) The after effects of the war left much of the county war-damaged. This bomb damage is believed to be at Shoreham. Many bombsites existed well into the 1970s. (*WanPs-0332*)

(*Opposite below*) Removing road blocks, Castle Street, Tonbridge, c.1945. (*WanPs-0347*)

The Grand Hotel Dover was damaged by German bombing on 11 September 1940. Enemy activity on that day consisted of one major attack between 1545 and 1645 hours comprising 250 German aircraft on the Kent Coast. Some thirty aircraft penetrated as far as London. Considerable damage was caused in Dover to houses, shops and Dover Priory railway station, as well as to the Grand Hotel. Seven people were killed, 122 seriously injured and 36 slightly injured as a result of the bombing. Located on the seafront at the end of Camden Crescent, it was finally demolished in 1951 by Frank Luck who paid Dover Corporation £1,000 for the salvage rights. *(WanPs-3119)*

Bibliography

From D-Day to VE Day, The Canadian Soldier, Jean Bouchery, Histoire & Collections.

Operation Neptune, Commander Kenneth Edwards RN, Collins, 1946.

The Last Ditch, David Lampe, Cassel & Company, 1968.

The Blitz Then and Now, Volume 2, *After the Battle*, 1988.

D-Day Fortitude – South Kent's Wartime Deception, John Raymond, Arts & Libraries Publications, 1994.

The ABC of British Cars, Graeme L. Greenwood, Ian Allen, 1947.

Wartime Editions of the *Dover and East Kent News* and the *Dover Express*.

Web Resources:

http://www.ibiblio.org (free information databases online).

http://crht.ca (Canadian Royal Heritage Trust).

http://www.britishpathe.com (British Pathe online).

http://www.dover-kent.com/Grand-Hotel.html (Dover Kent Archives).

Index

Notes

Notes

Notes

Notes

Notes